C. S. Lewis
and
Human
Suffering

Light among the Shadows

Marie A. Conn

HiddenSpring

Cover design by Trudy Gershenov
Book design by Lynn Else

Library of Congress Cataloging-in-Publication Data

Conn, Marie A., 1944–
   C.S. Lewis and human suffering : light among the shadows / Marie A. Conn.
      p. cm.
   Includes bibliographical references.
   ISBN-13: 978-1-58768-044-1 (alk. paper)
   1. Lewis, C. S. (Clive Staples), 1898–1963. 2. Suffering—Religious aspects—Christianity. I. Title.
   BX4827.L44C66 2008
   231'.8092—dc22

                                                                2007044993

Published in the United States by

HiddenSpring
an imprint of Paulist Press
997 Macarthur Boulevard
Mahwah, New Jersey 07430

www.hiddenspringbooks.com

Printed and bound in the
United States of America

C. S. Lewis
and
Human
Suffering

Contents

For Carrie, Tiffaney, Mary, and my Dad,
who died too young

and
for Regis,

who never stopped believing in me
and

for Mom,

whose struggle I was privileged to share

Preface

Carrie died in May. It was impossible to absorb the message left on my answering machine. Who was this Carrie who had died, and why did my department chair offer me such sympathy at her death? The only message I expected to receive of *my* Carrie, a student, was news of the birth of her baby, perhaps an invitation to the christening. But Carrie, beautiful, quiet, precious Carrie, had died from complications of childbirth. No, that couldn't be right. Women, young women, simply don't die in childbirth, not in America, not in the twenty-first century. But there it was. After a difficult pregnancy, Carrie's body did what she had willed it to do—carried Kaitlyn to term and delivered her safely—and then it could do no more. Carrie died just five days after holding her newborn daughter.

Less than a month after Carrie's death, a dear friend kissed her husband as he headed out for his usual Sunday-morning bike ride. She never saw him alive again. The heart attack was so sudden and so complete that Jim was gone before anyone could reach him. Sharon and Jim had always been people of deep faith, and Sharon remains a committed believer. But she was left with such wrenching pain that each day held new revelations of heartache.

My eighty-five-year-old mother's battle with cancer—a battle which should have taken her quickly—continued into its sixth year. Yet middle-aged Mary, with a loving husband and three devoted adult children, lost her battle with cancer in less than a year. The cancer came out of nowhere, attacking lungs that had never known smoke. Despite Mary's valiant and courageous fight, it swept her away before we could even absorb the seriousness of her condition.

Grief there is aplenty. What we do with that grief, how we cope with the blows dealt us by life, how we come to terms with mortality, our own and others'—all this is one of the most important experiences any of us will ever face. An approach to grief that acknowledges what we are going through, that allows us to grieve while protecting us from despair, is critical if we are to steer a steady course through the grief to the rest of our life. But learning to read the signposts that will conduct us safely through the journey of suffering and grief requires a guide.

One of the best guides on this journey is hardly unfamiliar. C. S. Lewis first published *A Grief Observed* more than forty years ago, but his thoughts, his naked honesty about his feelings after the death of his wife Joy Davidman, who had come into his life only after decades of bachelorhood, are as piercing and fresh as if he had just set them down today. Lewis's life before Joy is instructive, too. After his mother's death from cancer when he was just nine years old, Lewis drifted from the church of his birth and became a self-styled atheist. Lewis's experiences in the trenches of World War I reinforced his conviction that God, if God existed at all, was not someone whose acquaintance Lewis cared to pursue. He immersed himself in academic and scholarly pursuits, set up a new, albeit unusual, household, and took his first shaky steps on the way to publication. Years later, after embracing Christianity, Lewis answered questions about pain in traditional and conventional ways, speaking of God's will and of God's use of suffering to temper and sculpt us. But his unexpected love for Joy, her long and painful struggle with cancer, and finally her loss forced him to face the brutal truth of nearly overwhelming grief.

Preface

So, a mid-twentieth-century Oxford don from Ireland can help us explore the evolution of our own understanding of the role of suffering and death in our lives. C. S. Lewis had a sharp intellect, an endless curiosity, a gift for friendship, and an openness to truth. He urges us to let the heart go through its own seasons, find its own way, without platitudes or easy answers, but with honesty and faith.

~❧ ❧~

> Still I wish it could be forbidden that after a great man is dead, little men should scribble over him, who have not and must know they have not sufficient knowledge of his life and character to give them any key to the truth.[1]

A year after his friend Lewis had died, J. R. R. Tolkien wrote these words, provoked by an article about Lewis by one of his pupils. What would Tolkien have thought if he could foresee just how many "scribblings" would be written about Lewis—and about himself, for that matter—by people who did not know him? Which brings us to a key question: Why another book on C. S. Lewis? A complete bibliography of books about some aspect or other of Lewis's thought, never mind his own prodigious publications, would already take several pages.[2] And yet I am dissatisfied in one area of these other books; namely, the development of Lewis's consideration of the role and effects of suffering and death in human life.

More than forty years after his death, C. S. Lewis remains one of the most influential writers of recent history. Many Americans first come to know Lewis through his series of children's books, the Chronicles of Narnia, and as they mature, they continue to enjoy his many works. Lewis's experience of finding love late in life after decades of bachelorhood, and of suffering a tremendous sense of loss when that love was snatched away by an insidious cancer, found expression in his powerful little journal, *A Grief Observed*. My friend Sharon, mentioned at the beginning of this Preface, lost her forty-nine-year-old husband quite suddenly to a heart attack. She told me once that *A Grief Observed* was the only book she could read for a long time after Jim's death.

But that in itself serves to oversimplify Lewis as a man and as a Christian apologist. As Michael White observes, many readers "have managed to morph the real Jack Lewis into a version of himself even he would have had trouble recognizing." He enjoyed drinking and smoking, even after doctors advised him to stop. He was not celibate, and he enjoyed bawdy songs and stories.[3]

Even worse, the popular film *Shadowlands* has, in its most recent incarnation, reduced Lewis after his marriage to a naive, inexperienced man completely ignorant of many aspects of human life. Even a cursory reading of one of the many biographies available today (my preferred account is *Jack* by his longtime friend George Sayer) reveals a complex person, a child of nine who lost his mother to cancer, a World War I veteran, a good and true friend, a faithful brother—in other words, a normal human being who just happened to be one of the most talented and productive writers of the twentieth century.

This book seeks to explore Lewis's thoughts on the "why" of human suffering and, ultimately, of death, but it seeks to do the early Lewis more justice than he usually is granted. Starting with Lewis's *A Grief Observed* is tempting but intrinsically unfair, since that is the equivalent of reading the last page of a mystery, learning "whodunit," and then going back and looking at the clues to see how they fit into the solution.

When I first envisioned this project a few years ago, I suspected it would be, so to speak, a drama in two acts: the pre-Joy Lewis and the post-Joy Lewis. It did not take long to realize that even that approach did not take seriously Lewis's young adulthood.

Preface

This is essentially, therefore, an evolution in three broad
movements: Lewis the atheist, Lewis the Christian apologist, and
Lewis the husband and widower. The first movement begins with
Lewis's loss of his mother to cancer when he was nine years old and
extends beyond his experiences in World War I. Perhaps looking
back over those years, Lewis notes in *The Problem of Pain* that pain
is not a problem in the theological or philosophical sense for the
atheist, but only for one who is going to insist on the existence of
God. The second movement flows out of Lewis's midlife conversion experience. His Christian commitment became so complete
that he declared without hesitation that pain was "God's megaphone" to rouse us out of complacency, or God's "chisel" to perfect
our form. Then Joy Davidman entered and, too soon, left his life.
Lewis was shattered. The journey described in *A Grief Observed* has
its rightful place here as the third movement, the culmination but
not the sum total of this evolution of understanding.

This book will attempt to rescue Lewis from the "shadowlands" of his own fame and demythologize the great lover of myth. It
will demonstrate that the deep commitment to faith evident in so
many of Lewis's works grew out of an ordinary life lived with
extraordinary engagement. It will also connect Lewis's journey with
our own, suggesting that the honest suffering in *A Grief Observed* is
an alternative, "road not taken" approach to suffering of all kinds.

This book, however, does not worship at the Lewis shrine. In
fact, at one point in the research, I began to realize that, had we met,
Lewis and I would probably have disagreed on many things. But I
also gradually came to realize that this impression was due largely
to the respect verging on religious fervor with which many books
about Lewis were written. In those books, the real Lewis, the complex, multidimensional man behind the prolific publications, was in
danger of being lost completely.

This book will bridge the gap between the absolutely committed Christian of the published works and the struggling, ques-

tioning man who dealt with the doubts and problems common to all of us. Over the years of research that went into this project, I was struck by the irony of engaging in "biographical criticism" of a man who intensely disliked the genre. He felt it is too much about the writer and not enough about the writing.[4] But, in this case, it *must* be about the man behind the writing. Far from detracting from the power of his words, this book will lend them an honesty that can only enhance Lewis's reputation.

Acknowledgments

I would be remiss should I not acknowledge the support and encouragement of many people during the years I spent on this project. Regis Duffy, OFM, my professor, mentor, and friend, did not live to see the completed manuscript, but he was unfailing in his faith in me. I have referred to him with love as my best cheerleader.

Chestnut Hill College twice awarded me summer travel grants. The first enabled me to take part in a unique experience, the Oxford Round Table. While spending a week at Pembroke College, I was able to get reading credentials at the Bodleian Library and to visit sites associated with Lewis. The second grant enabled me to spend several days at the Marion Wade Center at Wheaton College in Illinois, the foremost American repository of original Lewis letters and other materials. I was also invited to participate in a conference at Wheaton and was pleased to meet the authors of some of the many books cited in this work.

During my time at Pembroke, I was lucky to contact Ron Brind of C. S. Lewis Tours (www.cslewistours.com). Ron was a boy in Headington, Oxford, when Joy and her sons moved in, and he remembers Douglas in particular as a childhood playmate. Ron's tour presented me with the opportunity to visit many sites in Oxford and Headington associated with Jack and Joy, from Magdalene College to some of Jack's favorite pubs to "The Kilns," his home for the last thirty years of his life. We also visited the church graveyard where Jack and his brother Warnie are buried, and the crematorium where Joy's ashes are marked by a poetic tribute from Jack.

Laura Schmidt, archivist at the Wade Center, has been unfailing in her willingness to clarify, explain, explore, and suggest—and to answer a question asked for the third time as if it were brand-new. Laura made me feel welcome when I was able to use the Center's reading room, and responded to every e-mail with a promptness that I can only hope to emulate with my own correspondents.

Here at Chestnut Hill College, Carol Consorto, our interlibrary loan librarian, did what she always does: attended to any and all of my requests graciously, quickly, and most efficiently. Carol leaves no proverbial stone unturned in finding obscure materials.

A friend and colleague from my days at another college, Christine Mihelich, IHM, agreed to read, critique, and comment on draft portions of this book. Christine is a professor of English and an admirer of Lewis, the perfect combination.

Finally, thanks are due to Jack and his Joy, for leading extraordinary lives and leaving behind an extraordinarily rich literary heritage.

Introduction

All My Road Before Me

The Man Behind the Books

On November 23, 1963, the day after his friend C. S.
Lewis died, British clergyman J. B. Phillips was watch-
ing television in Dorset, England, when he saw a vision
of Lewis sitting in a chair next to him. All the traces of
the debilitating prostate cancer that had killed Lewis
were gone. The searing grief Phillips had felt over his
friend's death was replaced by feelings of joy and peace
as Lewis reminded him: "It's not as hard as you think,
you know."[1]

A journalist once observed of Lewis that "in an age of easy
believism (and easy nonbelievism), cheap grace and oversimplifica-
tion of faith, Lewis has a muscular intellect that forces a reader to
focus on ultimate truths."[2] It is that "muscular intellect" that continues to serve those seeking meaning in the midst of grief.

Clive Staples Lewis, known to friends and family as Jack, was
born in Belfast on November 29, 1898. His father, A. J. Lewis, was
Welsh, sentimental and emotional; his mother, Flora August
Hamilton Lewis, a clergyman's daughter, was Norman and happy,
with an even disposition. Perhaps because of his father's influence,
Lewis later said that, until he met Joy Davidman, he had a fear of

1

emotions, which he found uncomfortable and embarrassing.[3] In later years, Lewis would distinguish between unfocused emotion and emotion transformed by discipline into art. Donald Glover notes a guiding principle of Lewis's criticism and art: "Art transmutes feeling into delight, giving it meaning and purpose, legitimizing it." Lewis seems to have been more comfortable with feelings in literature than in life.[4]

When Lewis was nine, his mother died and his life was changed forever. He and his brother Warner, known as Warnie, were sent to a brutal English boarding school. By the age of fifteen, Lewis had become a fervent atheist.[5] At nineteen, he was serving as a second lieutenant with the Somerset Light Infantry in the trenches of World War I, at one point capturing sixty German soldiers. His best friend was killed in the war and Lewis himself was badly wounded. Later, when the "war to end all wars" was followed by another world war, Lewis's was the second most-recognized voice in England after Winston Churchill.[6]

In 1925—twenty-five years before Lewis had met his wife— he experienced a conversion to what he called *joy,* a belief in God that was not yet necessarily a belief in Christianity. One night, in a discussion about myths, Lewis's good friend and colleague J. R. R. Tolkien said that all myths come from God and contain some of God's truth. Something happened that felt like a rush of wind, filling both of them with *joy.* Although remaining intellectually skeptical, Lewis did feel that this was some sort of message from God, and at the age of thirty he reluctantly joined the Anglican Church.

One of the most intriguing essays on Lewis is also one of the most modest, an account by the man who, for years, regularly drove Lewis to and from the train station, and anywhere else the don needed to go. In describing his first encounter with Lewis, A. Clifford Morris remembers that he was told to look for Dr. Lewis, "a portly gentleman who would be wearing a thick overcoat and a tribly hat with the brim turned down all round; he would also be carrying a walking-stick, would have a haversack on his back, be wearing glasses, and would look like a prosperous farmer."[7]

Luke Rigby agrees, describing Lewis as "usually rather shabby," wearing tweed jackets and flannel slacks, and smoking a pipe. Rigby says that this accurately portrayed Lewis's genuineness and warmth, but belied his depth and brilliance.[8]

These descriptions confirm the impression of Lewis given in his letters and his diaries. He seems to have been a very active, "regular" person who loved swimming, talking to a variety of people, walking, going to pubs, and so on. In other words, Lewis had a full, busy, and generally happy life.[9] He was, in the words of Jocelyn Gibb, "very much a whole man, one with a closely knit mind and certainly not dividing up into categorical departments." He could be formidable but had a good sense of fun. He had a scholarly mind, a remarkable memory, and a deep sense of truth.[10]

Kathleen Raine, who knew Lewis during his last years at Cambridge, described him this way:

> To meet [Lewis] was to know that here was a man of great learning, continuously kindled into life by imagination. He seemed to possess a kind of boyish greatness—an unique combination of qualities, for in him neither seemed to vitiate the other....For him learning was a joyful and inexhaustible game....In personal life he did not proselytize or persuade....Every conversation was an exploration, or a game with a shining ball flying through the air.[11]

As Lewis's regular driver, Morris got quite friendly with him, and their relationship continued even after Lewis's move to Cambridge since he came home to Oxford most weekends. According to Morris, Lewis was a great lover of nature, walks, and picnics. He also loved a joke. It was Morris who took Lewis home from the hospital on the night that Joy died; he was the first one to speak with him after her death. Morris described a long conversation that, he said, gave him a sense of intense sorrow and personal grief, but also of abiding faith.[12]

Morris found Lewis a "Christian gentleman,...a man who knew what he believed." Lewis did not use platitudes or shallow optimism. "What he said would have a welcome freshness, a new viewpoint, opening up attractive avenues for further exploration."[13]

More than one author has tried to explain Lewis's continuing appeal to so many readers. Glover feels one reason is Lewis's ability to "say religious things in an essentially nonreligious way." Lewis thought good fiction could "entice the reader beyond his understanding." Art and literature must be committed to moral truth, and so Lewis preferred "imaginative works with an underlying theme of spiritual significance to those of outright theology."[14] Glover goes on to say that Lewis "valued his readers' accessibility to new ideas,...felt his readers were better judges of the value of a literary work than critics and...his chief delight as a reader himself and then as an author was the compelling suggestiveness of a finely crafted story."[15]

Joy Davidman, a New Yorker who had corresponded with Lewis for nearly three years, finally met him in 1952, during her first trip to London. Eventually, mutual admiration turned to abiding friendship and finally to deep and romantic love. They were married first for convenience in 1956—Joy needed a way to remain in England—and the next year sacramentally. Sadly, by that time Joy had been diagnosed with a particularly nasty cancer, and although she enjoyed some years of remission, she died in 1960.

Jack later described the period following Joy's death as characterized not only by living every day in endless grief but also by *thinking* about living every day in endless grief. Using schoolboy notebooks, Jack kept a written journal of this period, soon published as *A Grief Observed*. In 1961, he himself was diagnosed with prostate cancer, but he already had kidney and heart problems that prevented surgery. Some say that Lewis dealt with his own impending death much more calmly than he had with Joy's. He died on November 22, 1963, less than a week before his sixty-fifth birthday and on the same day that the American president John Kennedy was assassinated.

Jack's obituary in the *New York Times* described him as a literary historian, Christian apologist, and author.[16] In 1946 Lewis had written some words which, in light of his later life, now seem strangely prophetic.

> We are not living in a world where all roads are radii of a circle and where all, if followed long enough, will therefore draw gradually nearer and finally meet at the center: [we are living] rather in a world where every road, after a few miles, forks into two, and each of those into two again, and at each fork you must make a decision.[17]

Lewis's war poem *Dymer* is discussed in chapter 2, but a passage from it seems to offer a fitting conclusion to this introduction:

> You, stranger, long before your glance can light
> Upon these words, time will have washed away
> The moment when I first took pen to write,
> With all my road before me—yet to-day,
> Here, if at all, we meet....[18]

1

Bits of a Life

A Look at C. S. Lewis

> He was an extremely amusing man with a sharp wit and
> an often acerbic tongue, he was jolly company....Most
> of all he had a tremendous gift for conveying complex
> ideas in a brilliantly clear fashion; he could write as he
> spoke, with a wonderfully warm, welcoming, encourag-
> ing voice.[1]

Lewis was more than an academic and a Christian apologist:
he was a writer of tremendous range.[2] Professor John Lawlor, a former student of Lewis, observed that within Lewis, "maddening
obstinacies and sword-sharp disclaimers co-existed with an untrou-
bled awareness of the highest order."[3]

Childhood

C. S. Lewis, who declared at four that he would only answer
to "Jack" or "Jacksie,"[4] described his background in his memoir,
Surprised by Joy: "I am a product of long corridors, empty sunlit
rooms, upstairs indoor silences, attics explored in solitude, distant
noise of wind under the tiles. Also, of endless books."[5]

C. S. Lewis and Human Suffering

Albert Lewis, Jack's father, was an Ulsterman with a temperament inherited from his Welsh ancestors: sentimental, passionate, mercurial. Jack's mother's ancestry was French, marked by mildness, freshness, and less reliance on rationality. Jack preferred his mother's heritage to his father's.[6] The family belonged to the Anglican communion of the Church of Ireland. Lewis's grandfather, vicar of the local church, often got highly emotional, even weeping, while preaching. This embarrassed the young Lewis and played a part in his later repudiation of his childhood faith, leading him to regard a spiritual worldview as silly.[7]

Jack described his mother as "spectacled, stout and keen on knitting," while his father was "generally grumpy and at home dressed in a scruffy jumper."[8] In distinguishing later between his "childhood" and his "boyhood," Lewis remembered the years with his mother as carefree and content. He felt secure and loved. This period ended with the death of his mother.[9]

The death of Jack's mother completely disintegrated his previously oversheltered and isolated life. She died on August 23, 1908, at the age of forty-six. Jack hated seeing his dead mother and hated the funeral as empty ritual.[10] Jack lost his paternal grandfather during this period, too. The double loss, combined with his father's changed manner, caused the boy to experience pessimism and depression; he was also bitter about the unanswered prayers for his mother's recovery.[11] White draws an interesting parallel between Lewis and Tolkien, who also lost his mother early (Tolkien's mother died at the age of thirty-four). Later, the two writers, perhaps in search of lost childhoods, created the imaginary worlds of Middle-earth and Narnia.[12] White believes Lewis's prolific writings allowed him to pour out repressed emotions, something he could not do verbally.[13]

Much that went into shaping the adult C. S. Lewis derived from the events of 1908. His character was moulded by the pain of loss, followed by the agony of isolation, the suppression of emotion, the claustrophobia of life at Little Lea [the family home in Belfast] and then the wrench away from all that was familiar.[14]

By 1911, Jack was completely taken up in his "Northerness," a fascination with myths and legends, which remained in him for life. This, too, was perhaps an escape:

He had embarked on a journey to a place where he would be untouched by the pain of memory. Here the dark, unpalatable tastes of the real world could not reach him. The world of books and music was not the world in which his mother was as dead as a stone; it was a land he could call his own, beyond interference.[15]

One of Jack's enduring relationships was his lifelong friendship with Arthur Greeves. In Greeves, the young Jack found a kindred spirit who also loved the sagas of the North. In an unpublished memoir, Warnie preserves his brother Jack's thoughts about his best friend:

It might seem that I had much to give [Arthur], and that he had nothing to give me. But this is not the truth. I could give the concepts, logic, facts, arguments, but he had feelings to offer, feelings which most mysteriously— for he was always very inarticulate—he taught me to share. Hence, in our commerce, I dealt in superficies, but he in solids. I learned clarity from him and failed, for all my efforts, to teach him arrogance in return.[16]

"It was Arthur [Greeves] who first prompted Jack to write about [joy]. For Lewis, [joy] was a sense, a feeling, a quality difficult to define but which he was sure lay at the heart of all great art."[17] *Joy* is "an unsatisfied desire which is itself more desirable than any other satisfaction." *Joy* is different from happiness and pleasure. Once someone experiences *joy,* he or she wants it again.[18] This *joy* is a sense of wonder at the center of all things that were dear to Jack. It was the cornerstone of Narnia and his later Christian faith.

In *Surprised by Joy,* Lewis discusses the great impact that Wagnerian music had on him, especially a bound edition of *Siegfried and the Twilight of the Gods,* illustrated by Arthur Rackham. The Norse gods, that "Northerness," taught Jack what disinterested worship was in a way that Christianity never had. "Sometimes I can almost think that I was sent back to the false gods there to acquire some capacity for worship against the day when the true God should recall me to Himself."[19]

Boyhood

Albert Lewis, unable to cope with his own grief at his wife's death, placed his sons in boarding schools. Lewis's experiences were disastrous. At Wynyard School in Surrey, which both Warnie and Jack agreed was a place of torture and degradation, Lewis later recalled first coming to serious but joyless faith. His was a legalistic approach to belief, and the God he envisioned was one of anger and wrath. As Downing puts it, "The lonely little boy imprisoned himself in a religion of guilt, not grace."[20] After a stay at Campbell College in Belfast, Lewis was sent to Cherbourg House in Worcestershire, a preparatory school for Malvern College. There, Lewis "became an unbeliever with a great sense of relief, not regret."[21] It was at this period that Lewis felt his atheism strengthened by what he would later describe as the "problem of pain": how a good and loving God could permit suffering.[22] Lewis did not believe there was a God, yet he resented God for not existing. He also resented this God who might or might not exist for creating such a flawed world.[23]

It is clear from *Surprised by Joy* that Lewis blamed his father for the miseries of school. Michael White, however, in discussing Lewis's memoir, observes: "And if Lewis's autobiography is shot through with poorly disguised bitterness towards the man, it is also clear that it was the raconteur and the confident, outspoken debater in him that he loved most and remembered best."[24] In later years, after Lewis became a don at Oxford, his five-hundred-pound salary finally allowed him to be free of the need of financial support from his father. This in turn made the father-son relationship better.

Finally, Jack was sent to a private tutor, William Kirkpatrick, at Great Bookham in Surrey. In "Kirk" or "Great Knock," Lewis had finally met his intellectual—and atheistic—match. Kirkpatrick deepened Lewis's dismissal of religion as irrelevant; Christianity was just one myth among many. The youthful Lewis dismissed his childhood experiences of *joy* as wish fulfillment and vowed never to be taken in again.[25] Yet Kirkpatrick recognized Jack's intellectual potential, and taught him how to learn using discipline and methodology. Lewis would later say that he learned, not atheism, which he had already embraced, but critical thinking and strict work habits from Kirkpatrick.[26]

It was also at Great Bookham that Lewis discovered the Scottish writer George MacDonald. MacDonald's *Phantastes* remained one of Lewis's favorite books until his death. From MacDonald, Lewis learned how to put complex concepts in the form of stories: "No concept was too difficult to portray as fiction, and that in fact, if handled skillfully, fiction is a wonderful medium through which a readership may be educated."[27]

MacDonald showed Lewis that he could satisfy both sides of his "divided" personality, his imagination and his intellect. Even as a young man, Lewis believed that poetry and the world of the imagination were "nearer to the truth than the world of the senses."[28]

"[Lewis's] tastes were essentially for what had magnitude and a suggestion of myth: the heroic and the romantic never failed to excite his imagination and although, at that time, he was something of a professed atheist, the mythically supernatural things in ancient epic and saga always attracted him."[29]

MacDonald also showed him that imagination, the dimension favored by Lewis, was, in fact, a valuable asset. Lewis now saw intellect, the organ of truth, and imagination, the organ of meaning, as complementary, not competitive. The imagination generates pictures, metaphors, and myths by which we understand the world; the intellect weighs, sifts, analyzes, and discerns the most suitable metaphors.[30]

Oxford

In 1916, Jack earned a scholarship in classics to University College, Oxford. However, having twice failed the Oxford Responsions (entrance exams), Jack would get to attend Oxford only after the war, when the university waived this requirement for servicemen. Lewis met his friend Paddy Moore when both were part of the cadet battalion at Keble College. Mrs. Moore and Paddy's sister Maureen had a great influence on Lewis after the war. [31] Lewis's war experiences are described in chapter 2.

Jack began living with Mrs. Moore and Maureen in 1919. Albert Lewis died after cancer surgery in 1929. Once Little Lea, the Lewis family home in Belfast, was sold, Jack was able to buy The Kilns, in Headington near Oxford, with the help of Warnie and Mrs. Moore.[32] Donald Glover described daily life at The Kilns this way: "At the Kilns, [Lewis] was a subject of Mrs. Moore's domestic tyranny and washed dishes and fed the chickens with an aplomb that worries many of his critics." But, Glover muses, perhaps Lewis had simply found with her the first "home" he had known since his mother's death.[33]

Bits of a Life

The exact nature of Lewis's relationship with Mrs. Moore has been dissected time and again. Lewis's longtime friend George Sayer thinks other writers make too much of Jack and Mrs. Moore. She was a mother figure and there was nothing odd in their relationship. Sayer recalls a remark Lewis once made: "She was generous and taught me to be generous, too. If it were not for her, I should know little or nothing about ordinary domestic life as lived by most people."[34]

Sayer credits life with the Moores with giving Lewis a more balanced preparation for his future career than Oxford alone could have offered. He learned to care about other people. He learned how to talk with ordinary people, expressing himself in direct, simple language. "Perhaps his life with the Moores made it more difficult for him to excel academically, but, far more important, it enabled him to become a great popular writer."[35] Over the years with the Moores, Lewis also came to an understanding of humanity, and of pain and suffering, that he might not have had, simply living as a bachelor don.

Lewis was elected a fellow of Magdalen College at Oxford in 1925, and met Tolkien in 1926. Tolkien was nearly seven years older, but both men had fought in the trenches of World War I and both adored language. Tolkien was less urbane than Lewis; he was also a husband and the father of four. Neither Lewis nor Tolkien ever really accepted the twentieth century. They shared an intellectual keenness and were soon each other's most trusted critic.[36] Together, Lewis and Tolkien gathered the Inklings, a group that met twice a week for readings and discussions. Lewis and Tolkien represent one of the most important literary friendships of the twentieth century.[37] The Inklings also gave Lewis a trusted circle of friends at Oxford, where he was often passed over for appointments because of his "lightweight" scholarship.

As he grew in both his teaching and his writing, Lewis displayed unusual qualities of mind. He was fluent in five or six languages. He possessed the power to think; the power "to make judgments and generalizations that lead the reader into new territory"; the power to write quickly, clearly, and forcefully. "His sentences are in homely English, and yet there is something Roman in the easy handling of clauses, and something Greek in their ascent from analogy to idea."[38]

Lewis left Oxford for Cambridge in 1954. The Cambridge English faculty created the professorship of medieval and Renaissance studies expressly for him. Because of Warren, and because they had only a life interest in The Kilns and couldn't sell it, Jack arranged to live at Cambridge Monday through Friday, returning to Headington for the weekend. Ironically, Jack moved from Magdalen College in Oxford to Magdalene College in Cambridge.[39]

Jack had begun his memoir, *Surprised by Joy: The Shape of My Early Life*,[40] in 1948. It was published in 1955. Sayer suggests that, rather than a true autobiography, the book is an exercise in catharsis, Lewis's way of getting rid of his past and his strained relationship with this father.[41]

Joy Davidman Lewis

Helen Joy Davidman, always called Joy, was born in New York City on April 18, 1915; her brother Howard arrived four years later. Her grandparents had been Orthodox Jews, but her parents had lapsed into atheism. Both her parents were social activists, both had degrees from City College of New York, both were involved with the public schools, and both enjoyed travel. They passed their love of reading on to their children. It was, in many ways, an idyllic childhood.[42] But that changed after Howard's birth, which had been a difficult one. Joy's mother went off to a dude ranch for an extended rest, leaving the young girl deprived of her mother's love and with a less-than-ideal relationship with her father.[43]

Bits of a Life

"There was absolutely nothing ordinary about Joy Davidman Lewis. Her IQ was unusually high; her memory nearly photographic. She read H. G. Wells's *Outline of History* at age eight and promptly announced her atheism."[44] Joy graduated from Hunter College at nineteen, and earned a master's from Columbia three semesters later. In 1934, Joy had seen a starving Depression-era orphan jump to her death, a memory that haunted the young writer.

> Indeed, the girl's suicidal plunge was in her mind continually, and her anger grew increasingly at the insanity and callousness of a society that dumped potatoes in the ocean, burned wheat, and poured lime on oranges, while millions of people were unemployed, malnourished, and forced to stand in soup lines and sort through refuse in garbage cans for sustenance.[45]

Disillusioned with the nation's economic system, Joy turned to Communism. She was attracted by the party's goals of full employment, equal opportunity, an end to discrimination against minorities, and the defeat of Fascism.[46] After teaching high-school students for two years, Joy went to Hollywood to try her hand at scriptwriting as part of the MGM program for young screenwriters, but found no success and quickly returned to New York. Joy's poem "Letter to a Comrade" won the Yale Series of Younger Poets award for 1938.[47]

Joy considered herself a sort of second-generation unbeliever, since her parents had already abandoned the Jewish faith of their upbringing. According to Lewis, this made Joy "extremely interesting to the reclaimed apostates of my own generation; the daring paradoxes of our youth were the stale platitudes of hers."[48] By the time she was twenty-five in 1940, she was on the staff of a weekly magazine; she had also published a book of poetry and a novel.[49]

Joy married William Lindsay (Bill) Gresham on August 2, 1942. Bill and Joy shared a passion for writing, an allegiance to Communism, and a strong social awareness, but they both needed something else. Bill provided Joy with a means of escape from her parents, while Joy gave Bill a purpose in life. Their first son David was born in 1944 and Douglas in 1945. But Bill drank too much and indulged in affairs. It was in this dark period that Joy turned to prayer and discovered the writings of C. S. Lewis.

The Gresham family turned to Christianity in 1947. Joy's personal account of her own return to religion has been told often.[50] Bill Gresham's drinking and womanizing had long plagued Joy's marriage, but a late-night phone call from him, telling of his fear that his mind was going, nearly destroyed her. It was at that moment, as she says so succinctly, "God came in."[51] Joy admitted she found no comfort in the experience—she was just as worried about Bill after as she had been before—but she did find new confidence built on God. Finding a return to Judaism unsatisfying, Joy turned to Christian sources. Francis Thompson's "The Hound of Heaven" and the works of C. S. Lewis were influential in her search. As she put it, "I snatched at books I had despised before....I went back to C. S. Lewis and learned from him, slowly, how I had gone wrong. Without his works, I wonder if I and many others might not still be infants 'crying in the night.'"[52] Dorsett observes that Joy has been obscured by Lewis's shadow: "Joy Davidman Lewis had a full and fascinating life before she ever met the renowned writer. Furthermore, she was markedly more important to him than their brief time together might suggest."[53]

Despite Joy's efforts to hold the marriage together, Bill started his affairs again, and she left him. By 1950, she had started a lively correspondence with Lewis. Ironically, Jack had entitled an autobiographical work *Surprised by Joy,* referring to what he had experienced with Tolkien but somehow prophetic nevertheless.

Joy came to England for the first time in 1952. She had been writing to Jack for two and a half years before they met for lunch at the Eastgate Hotel. Joy surprised Lewis by being so much like his male friends, drinking beer and holding her own in debates. These traits are probably what gave Joy entrée into Lewis's world, because he was a lifelong bachelor and felt completely at ease only among the men of his inner circle, "The Inklings." Jack seemed to be fascinated with the brash, outspoken, divorced American; many of Jack's friends never understood and never really accepted Joy's role in Lewis's life.[54]

"Ideologically, [Joy and Jack] were twins and after that first lunch Joy was totally convinced of her mission."[55] Lewis, in the Foreword to Joy's book *Smoke on the Mountain*, says Joy combined "a delicate precision of imagery [with] an occasional orotundity, a deep bell-like note."[56] Joy was very intellectual and enjoyed debates almost as much as Lewis himself did. It was while Joy and the boys were spending the Christmas holidays with the Lewises that Bill wrote asking for a divorce. In time, Joy did divorce Bill and moved with the boys to England permanently.

In the mid-1950s, Lewis left his position at Magdalen College in Oxford to take up a post at Magdalene College in Cambridge.[57] He observed that he was glad he would not be leaving Mary Magdalene, since by that time she knew him and his quirks so well. At the same time, Joy was experiencing extreme financial difficulties, due partly to a lack of promised support from Bill. Jack began to assume more and more responsibility for her and her sons, paying their rent and providing for the boys' education.[58]

Then Joy faced a new challenge. In 1956, the British Home Office refused to renew Joy's visitor visa. The only way to remain was to obtain British citizenship, and the only way she could do that was to marry a British citizen. Strangely, Jack stepped in and they were married secretly on April 23, 1956. The marriage was in name only, a civil affair without church sanction, a matter of expediency and friendship. Some authors do suggest, however, that Warnie already suspected that Jack felt much more for Joy than he was as yet willing to admit.

A mere six months later, life once again took an unexpected and disastrous turn. In October of 1956, on her way to answer the phone, Joy tripped and a bone in her leg snapped. She was diagnosed with cancer and during her initial hospitalization, Jack began to realize that his feelings for her had deepened. There were also the boys to think about. Although both Jack and Warnie were bachelors, because of their own mother's illness, they could truly understand what David and Douglas were going through. On Christmas Eve of 1956, Jack took another extraordinary step, having his marriage to Joy announced publicly in *The Times*. Jack now sought to have their marriage sacramentalized, but the bishop refused because of Joy's divorce; remarriage was forbidden by the Anglican Church.[59] A friend, Father Peter Bide, witnessed the marriage of Joy and Jack in Wingfield Hospital on March 21, 1957.

Then—remission. The next three years alternated between hope and discouragement. The cancer returned in 1959, but both Jack and Joy realized that they had to go on living. They actually managed a long-awaited holiday in Greece with friends in April of 1960, despite Joy's extreme weakness and nearly unremitting pain. In one of their constant discussions, Joy had remarked to Jack that even if they died at the same moment, side by side, the separation would be just as real. She also promised Lewis that she would come to him when he was on his own deathbed. Joy died on July 13, 1960, and was buried five days later.

Many people think they know Lewis and his relationship with Joy from the two versions of the movie *Shadowlands*. But the Lewis of the script is a poor reflection of the man himself. As Lyle Dorsett points out, both films are inaccurate because "in both films the producers distorted the facts for dramatic effect and to promote their own biases."[60] While Dorsett brings his own biases to his eval-

18

uation of the couple, he is right to warn against summing up either Joy or Jack according to Hollywood's interpretation.

Much has been debated about the "real" relationship between Jack and Joy. It cannot be denied, however, that, as different as they were in many ways, they also shared many things in common. They loved great literature and good writing, hated the city and preferred the country, and were critical of Americans.[61] They also enjoyed a good argument and were capable of sharp-tongued critiques.

Sayer observes:

> What impressed me most about their marriage was its natural quality. There was no striving to be something they were not, to be clever or even good. They just were. They accepted each other simply, naturally, without fret or fuss. They were kind to each other and unusually quick to grasp the nuances of each other's thoughts.[62]

2

The Loss of Conviction

World War I and Atheism

> For those whose spring ended before summer and those who remembered through their winter.[1]

In his "Elegy Written in a Country Churchyard," English poet Thomas Gray both honored and lamented the lives of the poor. He honored the inhabitants of the churchyard as human beings with inherent worth and dignity. But he lamented the loss of opportunity that has always been the plight of the poor. They never have the chance to develop their gifts. Gray was also well aware of the loss to society itself: these men and women never have the chance to put their gifts at the service of humanity:

> Perhaps in this neglected spot is laid
> Some heart once pregnant with celestial fire;
> Hands, that the rod of empire might have sway'd,
> Or waked to ecstasy the living lyre;
> But Knowledge to their eyes her ample page,
> Rich with the spoils of time, did ne'er unroll:
> Chill Penury repress'd their noble rage,
> And froze the genial current of the soul.[2]

The Loss of Conviction

While Gray was realistic about human nature—not every poor person might have waked the living lyre to ecstasy and some may indeed have become "little tyrants"—he nevertheless reminds us of one of the costs of any war. We lose a generation. We lose potential doctors and teachers, world leaders and social workers. And we lose artists and thinkers, poets and scholars, dreamers and theologians.

A group of my college friends has stayed in touch over the years. Whenever we get together, I have a living reminder of this cultural loss of World War I. One of my classmates, Noelie Kilmer Angevine, is Joyce Kilmer's granddaughter. Thanks to the war, Noelie never knew her grandfather. Isaac Rosenberg, hailed by critics as an emerging poetic genius, also died in World War I, as did John McCrae, author of the poignant poem "In Flanders Field." The list goes on.

But many of these creative spirits served and survived, marked forever by their experiences of the war. F. Scott Fitzgerald, convinced he was about to die, completed the first version of what would become his debut novel, *This Side of Paradise*. Fitzgerald soon became known as the premier spokesman for the "Lost Generation," those who came of age during World War I. Ernest Hemingway served as an ambulance driver. So war takes away, but war also leaves a creative remnant. C. S. Lewis is, thankfully, part of the creative remnant of World War I.

C. S. Lewis has often been described as pessimistic. Armand Nicholi finds in one of Lewis's letters, written some thirty years after the war, strong evidence that the war was one of the key factors behind this pessimism. As we have already seen, Lewis became a self-described atheist in early adulthood. In the letter in question, Lewis writes that the loss of his mother when he was nine, unhappiness in school, and his participation in war were the bases of both his pessimism and his atheism.[3] The implications of that view and his later experience of conversion, which Lewis called *Joy,* were seminal to his prodigious lectures and writings.

In May of 1939, C. S. Lewis wrote to Dom Bede Griffiths. (The abbreviations are Lewis's.)

> My memories of the last war haunted my dreams for years. Military service, to be plain, includes the threat of *every* temporal evil; pain and death wh. we fear from sickness; isolation from those we love wh. is what we fear from exile; toil under arbitrary masters, injustice and humiliation, wh. is what we fear from slavery; hunger, thirst, cold and exposure wh. is what we fear from poverty. I'm not a pacifist....but the flesh is weak and selfish and I think death wd. be much better than to live through another war.[4]

Lewis was called to service just as he was beginning his studies at Oxford University.[5] He had to move out of University College and into Keble College, which had been set up as a military barracks. "Many of the fifteen thousand or more students who were at the university during a normal term had already died in France during the first two-and-a-half years of the war, and those still alive were now mired in mud in some godforsaken trench or lying wounded in hospital."[6]

It was at Keble that Lewis met Edward "Paddy" Moore, his roommate. Lewis eventually became a second lieutenant and served in the trenches in France. In this, he was, as one author described him, "a representative young man from the period."[7] Lewis was part of the Somerset Light Infantry, he was part of the so-called "Lost Generation," and he was an atheist. The war shattered his early assumptions about life and the world. He would spend much of the rest of his life coming to terms with those lost assumptions and attempting to forge new ones.

Serving in the war was considered the only patriotic choice. Lewis and his brother Warnie both served, even though, for a time at least, their status as Irishmen could have exempted them. Poets like Rupert Brooke ennobled the war. Later writers, like Lewis, called the war into question, partly because it had silenced so many of Britain's sons like Brooke himself.[8]

Lewis loved the old, the stable, the secure. He was a lover of Northern myths and classical writers. The war threatened all this. The war, in fact, challenged Lewis's assumptions so deeply that, after it was over, he took his initial degree in philosophy, not literary criticism.

Lewis found parallels between his experiences in war and the death of his mother when he was nine. "Everything he encountered at the Front was a greater disorientation than Lewis had previously known; these phenomena forced his mind back to the images and associations that surrounded his mother's death. It was during that earlier trauma that he had first shaped his means of coping."[9]

Although he tended to romanticize the war in his letters, Lewis still had vivid memories of it decades later as World War II approached. He had endured horrendous conditions in the trenches in France, especially in the winter. Worse, he had become, as most soldiers do, "uncivilized" in the war, capable of doing things they would have otherwise thought impossible. Ironically, his experience of war was much more dangerous and harsh than was Warnie's, even though Warnie was a career soldier.

Time in the hospital with trench fever gave Lewis a respite to read and write, but also gave him time to think about the war and the possibility of his own death. The horrors he witnessed would emerge in later writings; prominent among the images would be corpses in strange postures, written about in *Surprised by Joy*.[10] In a letter to his lifelong friend Arthur Greeves, Lewis lamented the innocence he was losing to war: "Shall we ever be the same again?"[11]

C. S. Lewis and Human Suffering

Lewis was severely wounded in April of 1918, hit by three shell fragments, two of which were not removed until 1944.[12] Being incapacitated brought the possibility of being helpless should the Germans attack. In *Surprised by Joy*, Lewis remembered the experience: "I felt no fear and certainly no courage. It did not seem to be an occasion for either....It was not even interesting."[13] Years later, in a conversation with Lewis, Leo Baker, an Oxford colleague and fellow veteran, asked him if he had been frightened in France. Lewis famously remarked: "All the time, but I never sank so low as to pray."[14] His letters to Greeves are filled with the longing for his prewar happiness. "You, who have never lost that life, cannot understand the longing with which I look back to it."[15] He also seemed to exhibit symptoms of "shell shock," today's post-traumatic stress disorder, and was troubled by nightmares for years. Later, Lewis disapproved of the great jubilation at the war's end, mindful of all the lost young men. His friend Paddy Moore had been killed in France. That loss, together with Albert Lewis's decision not to come and visit his son in the hospital, caused Lewis to become more attached to Mrs. Moore.[16] Lewis was demobilized on December 27, 1918, and returned to Oxford on January 13, 1919, taking rooms in University College.[17]

After the war, Lewis saw a division between the spiritual world and the material world, the material world being a place of horror intent on destroying the spiritual. The reality of war challenged the mythical world Lewis so loved in literature. His wounds spared him the terrible times his unit later went through, but he grieved mightily for his dead comrades. His book of war poetry, *Spirits in Bondage,* chronicles the trauma of war and its effects on him.[18] Gilchrist, discussing the poems, sees the Lewis who wrote them as "...a young soldier who was being treated to visions of agony and death on a daily basis, and was intent on killing men in the trenches opposite his own."[19] His poem "Apology" laments that he could not "build a heaven of dreams in a *real* hell." His "Ode for

New Year's Day" laments the death of the "Good," which has been replaced by the evil God who allows all of war's destruction: "The sky above is sickening, the clouds of God's hate cover it." The last poem, "Death in Battle," conveys "the delight that will come after death and contrasts the beauty of the afterlife with the corruption of war."[20] His later full-length narrative poem, *Dymer,* explores war's trauma even more directly and thoroughly.[21] His diary of June 18, 1921, records that Lewis woke up in a state of misery for no apparent reason and found himself in tears.[22] *Dymer* was his attempt to exorcise the demons of war.

As late as 1955, in *Surprised by Joy,* Lewis was still unable to understand, or at least to communicate, his feelings about the war and its impact on him. He used detachment in describing his time in the trenches. White notes:

> As a soldier, [Lewis] had adopted an alien and quite temporary "survival person," and unlike many of those who survived the war and later became writers, he had no wish to draw on what he saw and felt in France and to write about it directly….He never made mental links between the experiences of late 1917 and early 1918 and his own literary imaginings.[23]

David Downing, however, finds the section of *Surprised by Joy* that deals with the war full of unforgettable images: trenches knee-deep in water; vast, cratered landscapes with no grass; mutilated soldiers; corpses frozen in a sitting position.[24] White also describes the spiritual impact of the war on Lewis:

> Like many young intellectuals of the time, in the immediate aftermath of the war Lewis found himself in a spiritual vacuum. Some men had actually found God in the trenches, but a great many others had lost any ortho-

25

dox faith they may once have possessed. Lewis was in the second category. By the time he returned to Oxford after the war, any religious feeling he had harboured had withered away to absolutely nothing.[25]

On June 3, 1918, Lewis wrote to Arthur Greeves from Endsleigh Palace Hospital in London, saying: "I believe in no God, but I do believe that I have in me a spirit, a ship, shall we say, of universal spirit; and that, since all good and joyful things are spiritual and non-material, I must be careful not to let [this] matter...get too great hold on me, and dull the one spark I have."[26]

Again, on September 12, Lewis wrote from Ashton Court, near Bristol: "*Spirits in Bondage* [was] mainly strung around the idea...that nature is wholly diabolical and malevolent and that God, if He exists, is outside of and in opposition of the cosmic arrangement."[27]

But, on another level, Lewis was aware from the beginning of the impact the war had had on him. In a 1918 letter to his father Albert, Lewis said he could "still perceive his uniform's fittings under his scholar's dress."[28] He was only about twenty-six when he began to feel like an old man: "So many of his generation had passed on that he must have felt with others in that day that only a scarred remnant remained."[29]

Gilchrist defines war literature as that which "records the shattering of assumptions and the consequent trauma that arises from war. It may also delineate the rebuilding of those assumptions."[30] War literature need not refer to battles directly or even at all. In *Spirits in Bondage* and in *Dymer,* Lewis looked at the devastation caused by war, and questioned the nature of a God who could allow such devastation to occur. Coincidentally, the ideal world that is so lamented by Lewis was reflected years later in J. R. R. Tolkien's *Ring* trilogy. Tolkien, a close friend and colleague of Lewis's, was also in the war. No wonder, then, that at the end of the trilogy, the elves leave humanity behind.[31]

In *Dymer,* Lewis evoked the experience of battle, the sound of shells and machine-gun fire. The poem describes the war's destruction of the world. Lewis also seemed to be reliving the guilt of the soldier who is forced to kill; soldiers both kill enemies and survive friends. "*Dymer* is the moment when Lewis gathers his courage...and plunges into the depths of his trauma....He confronted his war, moved toward survival, and toward the possibilities that lay in his future."[32]

Years later, after losing his beloved wife Joy, whom he found only after decades of bachelorhood, Lewis described grief, "like a bomber circling round and dropping its bombs each time the circle brings it overhead; physical pain is like the steady barrage on a trench in World War One, hours of it with no let-up for a moment."[33]

Lewis's war experiences gave him knowledge of grief, loss, and human atrocities. Those experiences stayed with him throughout his life and influenced his writing and thinking even after his conversion to Christianity. Later, as World War II approached, Lewis wrote to Dom Bede Griffiths that perhaps ceasing to exist would be a better option than experiencing another war.[34] Listen to "French Nocturne," the second poem in *Spirits in Bondage*:

> Long leagues on either hand the trenches spread
> And all is still; now even this gross line
> Drinks in the frosty silences divine,
> The pale, green moon is riding overhead.
> The jaws of a sacked village, stark and grim,
> Out on the ridge have swallowed up the sun,
> And in one angry streak his blood has run
> To left and right along the horizon dim.
> There comes a buzzing plane: and now, it seems

C. S. Lewis and Human Suffering

Flies straight into the moon. Lo! Where he steers
Across the pallid globe and surely nears
In that white land some harbour of dear dreams!
False, mocking fancy! Once I too could dream,
Who now can only see with vulgar eye
That he's no nearer to the moon than I
And she's a stone that catches the sun's beam.
What call have I to dream of anything?
I am a wolf. Back to the world again,
And speech of fellow brutes that once were men
Our throats can bark for slaughter: cannot sing.

3

Conviction Rediscovered

Lewis's Conversion

You must picture me alone in that room in Magdalen, night after night, feeling, whenever my mind lifted even for a second from my work, the steady, unrelenting approach of Him whom I so earnestly desired not to meet. That which I greatly feared had at last come upon me. In the Trinity Term of 1929 I gave in, and admitted that God was God, and knelt and prayed: perhaps, that night, the most dejected and reluctant convert in all England.[1]

The complex combination of Lewis's loss of his mother, his unfortunate school experiences, and his experience of war had left him a self-described atheist, with no use at all for organized religion. He distinguished religion from morality, which, in his view, was an innate human obligation.[2]

Lewis's conversion to Christianity happened gradually, between 1926, when *Dymer* was published, and 1931. Sayer believes that, without that gap, Lewis would not have become a mature Christian; he would, in Sayer's words, have lacked "imaginative sympathy and understanding."[3]

Jack grew to distrust psychology and introspection. He desired a religion with an objective, traditional morality. "By 1926 he was a practicing theist who had no belief in the gospel story or in the doctrine that Jesus Christ is the Son of God." A conversation with T. D. Weldon, a tutor at Magdalen whom Jack did not like, shocked him. Weldon asserted that there was, in fact, good historical evidence for the truth of the gospel story. Jack examined the evidence himself and from "this time onward, he felt under pressure to believe."[4]

In 1922, Lewis met Nevill Coghill, intelligent, well-informed, *and* "a Christian and a thorough-going supernaturalist."[5] Lewis was beginning to see that what he had left behind actually had value: "The things I assert most vigorously are those I resisted long and accepted late." He liked the writers MacDonald, Chesterton, Spenser, Milton, and especially seventeenth-century poet George Herbert, *despite* their Christianity—but began to realize that perhaps he liked them *because of* it. He found non-Christian writers dull and thin; twisting a line from the *Song of Roland,* he said, "Christians are wrong, but all the rest are bores." Even so, Lewis still did not examine Christianity itself.[6]

Lewis enjoyed reading religious authors. For example, in *Surprised by Joy,* Lewis described his unexpected liking of G. K. Chesterton's writings, which, he said, laid "traps everywhere" for a "sound Atheist." Lewis observed, "God is, if I may say it, very unscrupulous."[7]

The French philosopher Henri Bergson was also influential in Lewis's move away from atheism. Bergson's writings led Lewis to an idea of necessary existence; that the universe—although not yet "God" for him—is not just an arbitrary alternative to nothingness. There's no sense cursing or blaming the universe, since we are all a part of it: "One must...'accept' the universe, totally, with no reservations, loyally." Lewis called this "Stoic Monism...the philosophy of my New Look." It gave him a great sense of peace, obviating any idea of compromise with reality.[8]

Although Lewis at this point had to admit that there seemed to be some logic or mentality to the universe, he still managed to avoid theism: "There were in those days all sorts of blankets, insulators, and insurances which enabled one to get all the conveniences of Theism, without believing in God." Lewis called this "a religion that cost nothing." There was nothing either to fear or to obey. Heaven was there, but no one could reach it. "It is more important that Heaven should exist than that any of us should reach it."[9]

Lewis saw a distinction between *enjoyment*—experiencing something directly—and *contemplation*—thinking about the experience. He applied this distinction to *joy*: one could *enjoy* the desirable mental state, but should seek to *contemplate* the deeper reality. He began to wonder if that deeper reality might be God.[10]

In *Surprised by Joy,* Lewis explained his new understanding of *joy* and the steps in his conversion, steps he likened to chess moves. Chesterton's *Everlasting Man* provided Lewis with "the whole Christian outline of history set out in a form that seemed to [him] to make sense." He became aware of a completely free choice to open up or not; he chose to open up. On a bus ride from Madgdalen to Headington in 1929, he got on an unbeliever and got off believing that an absolute spirit or God did exist.[11] Downing describes Lewis on that bus as suddenly feeling challenged to open a door. The door later became "a symbol of giving up one's freedom, allowing oneself to be drawn in and to make a commitment."[12]

In the Trinity (summer) Term of 1929, Lewis gave in, admitted that God was God, and knelt and prayed, although he considered himself a "reluctant convert."[13] This conversion was to theism, not yet to Christianity. Furthermore, there was at yet no connection between God and *joy.* This God might even demand the surrender of *joy.* Lewis did not yet believe in an afterlife. He saw his unbelief as a blessing, because making an afterlife central to a religion can corrupt it. Goodness was meant to be disinterested, with no thought of reward or punishment. God is God and is to be obeyed whether God has power over us or not.[14]

Later, Lewis would continue to insist that eternal life is "no mere bribe," but the natural fulfillment of Christian fidelity during life. This awareness comes to us gradually: "Poetry replaces grammar, gospel replaces law, longing transforms obedience, as gradually as the tide lifts a grounded ship."[15] He went on to say that, while some parts of religion may seem puzzling or even repellent, we must be willing to grapple with them and try to find meaning in them. The major promise of eternal life is that we will be with Christ. All the other "bits" are meant to keep us from making this first promise overly concrete.[16]

He started to go to church regularly, but was still anti-ecclesiastical. He accepted some Christian concepts, but felt quite uneasy about others. "He had no understanding of the sacramental system and could not see the relevance of concepts similar to those found in pagan mythology—for instance, the ideas of sacrifice, propitiation, the shedding of blood, communion, and redemption."[17]

Lewis was not looking for the "one true" religion, but the one in which religion had reached its maturity; he felt this might be either Hinduism or Christianity. Eventually, he came to believe that Christianity seemed to have the greater maturity and historical claim. A pivotal moment was a conversation he had on September 19, 1931, with J. R. R. Tolkien and Hugo Dyson, during an after-dinner stroll around Addison's Walk in Oxford. Unlike Lewis, who loved myths but regarded them as untrue, Tolkien insisted myths originated in God and contained, in some form, God's truth. Tolkien went on to say that the Christian myth was invented by God, a God whose dying could transform Jack, if only he would "plunge in." After Tolkien left, Dyson talked about how Christianity works for the believer. "The believer is put at peace and freed from his sins. He receives help in overcoming his faults and can become a new person."[18] Together, the two friends made Jack see that the Christian myth was real and true. Lewis later said that passing from believing in God to definitely believing in Christ was a result of this conversation. A few days later, on September 22, 1931,[19] sitting in the sidecar of Warnie's motorcycle on a drive to the zoo at Whipsnade, Lewis made the leap: "When we set out I did not believe that Jesus Christ is the Son of God, and when we reached the zoo I did."[20]

Lewis discussed this experience with his friend Arthur Greeves in two letters, dated October 1 and October 18, 1931. In the first, Lewis was quite explicit: "How deep I am just now beginning to see: for I have just passed on from believing in God to definitely believing in Christ—in Christianity....My long night talk with Dyson and Tolkien had a good deal to do with it." In the second letter, however, Lewis said he might have been a bit hasty, that he might not have moved as far as the previous letter indicated. His difficulty was not so much in believing a doctrine as in knowing what a doctrine means. He was particularly baffled by the meaning of redemption: "in what sense the life and death of Christ 'saved' or 'opened salvation' to the world....What I couldn't see was how the life and death of Someone Else (whoever he was) 2000 years ago could help us here and now—except in so far as his *example* helped us."[21]

What Dyson and Tolkien had made Lewis see is that he did not resist the idea in any of the pagan stories, but only in the gospels. They somehow got him to accept that "the story of Christ is simply a true myth: a myth working on us in the same way as the others, but with this tremendous difference that *it really happened*."[22] So, this critical conversation helped Lewis deal with the dichotomy he had always seen between imagination and intellect, spirit and matter. Lewis came to believe that God is above nature as its Creator. "In this view humans need not spurn nature as evil or worship it as divine, but rather value nature as a part of creation as we ourselves are."[23]

C. S. Lewis and Human Suffering

Becoming a Christian did not diminish Lewis's doubts about church services, but it did diminish the importance of *joy* as he had previously understood it. *Joy* only pointed to something outside of itself. In retrospect, Lewis began to realize that his longing for the joy of childhood—toy garden, mountain views—had been a replacement for religious experience; only later did he see this as the beginning of *joy* in the Christian sense, a longing for union with God.[24] "When we are lost in the woods the sight of a signpost is a great matter....But when we have found the road and are passing signposts every few miles, we shall not stop and stare."[25]

The same sentiments are evident in a letter to Greeves dated November 8, 1931. In the letter, Lewis suggested that Christianity appealed to him less than paganism because paganism was the first thrilling encounter, whereas Christianity was the abiding reality. He likened it to the difference between first falling in love and then living the married life. He admitted, however, that it was necessary to move forward, rather than to try and recapture that first thrill.[26] Someone who had heard Lewis preach described his reaction to it: "Here, you feel even when reading, and you felt ten times more so when listening, was a man who had been laid hold of by Christ and who enjoyed it."[27]

"It was this union of rigorous critical intellect with rich poetic imagination that...gave Lewis's Christian apologetics such an extraordinary force." Lewis never really thought much about the institutional church. His religion was decidedly unecclesiastical. The externals of worship wearied him. Lewis was perhaps never able to reconcile the mythmaker and poet with the philosopher and moralist.[28]

"Lewis was a private person; he called his soul his own; he did not pursue pleasure as a matter of course; most of his time he spent avoiding suffering."[29]

34

When you ask me to "pray for you,"...I don't know if you are serious, but the answer is, I do. It may not do you any good, but it does me a lot, for I cannot ask for any change to be made in you without finding that the very same [change] needs to be made in me, which pulls me up and also by putting us all in the same boat checks any tendency to priggishness.[30]

Jack's conversion was the beginning of his career as a Christian novelist and popular theologian. His change of world-view occurred when he was thirty-one. "The change revolutionized his life, infused his mind with purpose and meaning, and dramatically increased his productivity; it also radically altered his values, his image of himself, and his relationship to others."[31]

Glover emphasizes, however, that, even before his conversion, Lewis "was articulate, brilliant, witty, and dedicated to his teaching career." He had a full and satisfactory life. Lewis's development as a writer was an evolution, not a sudden "conversion." And his appeal is not just that he is a "Christian writer," Glover warns: "It is a mistake to presume that...Lewis suddenly saw all literature as somehow nascently Christian." Lewis was, after all, a rational, shrewd literary critic.[32]

Austin Farrer regards Lewis as a natural apologist, one who could answer an attack or refute a criticism: "Lewis was an apologist from temper, from conviction, and from modesty. From temper, for he loved an argument. From conviction, being traditionally orthodox. From modesty, because he laid no claim either to the learning which would have made him a theologian or to the grace which would have made him a spiritual guide."[33]

Farrer goes on to say that Lewis's strength was not in the explanation of doctrines but in detecting fallacy in objections to belief and in making others see, as he so clearly did, the superiority of orthodox tenets:

C. S. Lewis and Human Suffering

> The great value of Lewis as an apologist was his many-sidedness....Though argument does not create conviction, the lack of it destroys belief. What seems to be proved may not be embraced, but what no one shows the ability to defend is quickly abandoned. Rational argument does not create belief, but it maintains a climate in which belief may flourish.[34]

Farrer finds *Miracles* and *The Problem of Pain* the most direct examples of Lewis's apologetic writing. He argues that other popular Lewis treatises are not, in fact, apologetic. *The Screwtape Letters, The Great Divorce,* and *Mere Christianity* are plain expositions, imaginative approaches to doctrine, and *Pilgrim's Regress* and *Surprised by Joy* lay out an intellectual history of Lewis's experience of conversion. Farrer points out Lewis's greatest strength as an apologist: "Muddled minds read him, and found themselves moving with delight in a world of clarity."[35] Referring to what he considered the overly elaborate doctrines of, for example, transubstantiation and consubstantiation, Lewis reminded readers that "the command, after all, was Take, eat: not Take, understand."[36]

Lewis's lack of theological credentials seemed to vex the English, who wished he would stick to literary criticism, but it appealed to Americans. *The Screwtape Letters,* for example, was popular because it combined faith and wit. Americans also saw Lewis as not having any real vested interest in religion. So, he could appeal to readers all along the Christian spectrum. Chad Walsh says the attraction came from the readers' desire for "a religious faith which would have its roots sunk deep in the main Christian tradition but which would not do violence to their intellects and knowledge." Such readers wanted orthodoxy but not fundamentalism. They found what they wanted in Lewis.[37]

Lewis's conversion did bring into his life one of his great friendships, that with Charles Williams. Williams, an editor at

Oxford University Press, came to Oxford in 1939, when the Press moved out of London due to the war.[38] In 1945, Charles Williams died. This devastated Lewis. Coghill expresses the opinion that, "Williams was the only one of us, except perhaps Ronald Tolkien, from whom Lewis learnt any of his thinking."[39] Jack's faith helped him through his pain. He sensed Williams' continued presence. "For him it somehow made the next world more real, and what he saw as one's inevitable destiny to go there had become something less frightening to contemplate."[40]

Lewis's *The Great Divorce: A Dream* takes its title from the division between those who choose to believe in God and obey God's will and those who prefer their own desires. According to Sayer, the book was a tribute to George MacDonald, a universalist. In it, Lewis tried to reconcile universalism, which he did not believe but thought possible, with various other Christian ideas, such as predestination, purgatory, and a particular judgment. So, Lewis made hell a permanent state for those who choose to stay there, and "purgatory for those who want to leave and are prepared to make the necessary sacrifice of self." Hell is not punishment but God's attempt at the ultimate conversion of lost souls.[41]

Downing observes that one of Lewis's favorite postconversion themes was "learning to accept what is given and to conform one's will to reality, rather than insisting on one's own way and trying to bend reality to one's will."[42] Downing also summarizes Lewis's journey to conversion as a movement from popular realism to philosophical idealism to pantheism to theism and finally to Christianity. Lewis's incisive mind demanded ever-clearer concepts of the Absolute—from vaguely defined (idealism) to the immanent soul of the cosmos (pantheism) to an Absolute apart from human reality (theism). He also needed a belief system with an ethical underpinning.[43]

Lewis himself was quite clear on this last point: "The Moral Law doesn't give us any grounds for thinking that God is 'good' in the sense of being indulgent, or soft, or sympathetic. There's nothing indulgent about the Moral Law. It's as hard as nails. It tells you to do the straight thing and it doesn't seem to care how painful, or dangerous, or difficult it is to do."[44]

Lewis also insisted that, although Christianity may bring comfort, it "doesn't begin in comfort." He insisted that it begins in the dismay we feel when we realize how far short of God's ideal we are constantly falling. We must go through that dismay before we have a right to the comfort.[45]

In his preface to an edition of Lewis's *God in the Dock*, Walter Hooper makes this observation: "Lewis struck me as the most thoroughly *converted* man I ever met. Christianity was never for him a separate department of life; not what he did with his solitude;...his whole vision of life was such that the natural and the supernatural seemed inseparably combined."[46]

4

The Problem of Pain

All Nonsense Questions Are Unanswerable

[Prayers in time of anguish] are themselves a form of anguish. Some people feel guilty about their anxieties and regard them as a defect in faith. I don't agree at all. They are afflictions, not sins. Like all afflictions, they are, if we can so take them, our share in the Passion of Christ. For the beginning of the Passion—the first move, so to speak—is in Gethsemane....The prayer in Gethsemane shows that the preceding anxiety is equally God's will and equally part of our human destiny.[1]

The question of human pain, suffering, and grief has provided the basis for much of the world's literature; the question is ancient, contemporary, timeless. For example, *The Epic of Gilgamesh* of ancient Babylonia is as fresh and poignant today as when it was first composed some five thousand years ago. Philosophers and theologians have wrestled with the problem of human suffering in succeeding generations since the days of ancient Greece. And yet, when C. S. Lewis asks himself, in *A Grief Observed,* whether a mortal can "ask questions which God finds unanswerable," he responds

39

that they can quite easily, since all nonsense questions are unanswerable.[2]

Much earlier than *A Grief Observed,* some years after his conversion, Lewis had written a treatise entitled *The Problem of Pain.* Lewis claimed that the sole purpose of the book was to "solve the intellectual problem raised by suffering."[3] In it, he pointed to the importance of support in times of suffering or sorrow: "When pain is to be borne, a little courage helps more than much knowledge, a little human sympathy more than much courage, and the least tincture of the love of God more than all."[4] He also acknowledged that thinking about pain and about the meaning of pain in order to write a book about it is different from actually experiencing it. After reading a chapter of the manuscript to the Inklings, Jack wrote to his brother:

> If you are writing a book about pain and then get some actual pain as I did from my rib, it does not either, as the cynic would expect, blow the doctrine to bits, nor as a Christian would hope, turn into practice, but remains quite unconnected and irrelevant, just as any other bit of actual life does when you are reading or writing.[5]

As an atheist, Lewis had acknowledged that humans are conscious of pain, in birth, in life, and in dying. We can also anticipate pain and even foresee our own death. Since at that time Lewis rejected a benevolent God, he saw human history as largely a story of people inflicting pain on each other. Using the analogy of wood, Lewis says that it warms at a distance, but burns when too close. "The permanent nature of wood which enables us to use it as a beam also enables us to use it for hitting our neighbour in the head."[6]

This Lewis saw Christianity as "a catastrophic historical event" that created, rather than solved, the problem of pain. After all, pain "would be no problem unless, side by side with our daily experience of this painful world, we had received what we think a good assurance that ultimate reality is righteous and loving."[7] Pain is an evil, but may sometimes be a justifiable or necessary evil. Pain can be morally instructive.[8] So the "problem" of pain lies in seeing honestly the suffering of the world, and yet still believing that goodness and suffering are not contradictory.[9]

Before he ever met his wife Joy, Lewis had known suffering. Besides enduring his mother's death, his father's distance, and the horrors of war, Lewis also lived with his dear brother Warnie's alcoholism, which led to many hospitalizations, and with Mrs. Moore's declining health, which made her personality increasingly more difficult.[10] So Lewis had as much right as anyone to examine the "problem of pain."

Simply stated, the problem is this: God is good, so God's creatures *should* be happy. God is almighty, so God's creatures *can* be happy. And yet, God's creatures more often than not experience pain of varying degrees throughout their lives. Lewis apparently felt that God *meant* us to be happy, but humans interfered with the divine plan. He felt that most of our suffering comes from other humans, so we have to explore why we treat each other so badly. Lewis saw free will as essential, since the only true happiness is freely choosing a loving relationship with God.[11]

Lewis said that God differs from us the way a perfect circle differs from a childish attempt to draw a circle. He said that God's goodness means Love, while *we* think that God's goodness means Kindness. Kindness would like to escape suffering, but Love allows it for the sake of moral growth. We want, not a Heavenly Father, but a Heavenly Grandfather. God gives us what we need, not always what we want. God has, in Lewis's view, "paid us the intolerable compliment of loving us, in the deepest, most tragic, most inexorable sense." The goal is not our happiness, but our ultimate perfection so that God can love us without impediment.[12] Furthermore, even if omnipotent, God will not do something that makes no sense; for example, stop nature's functioning. God's goodness is not indulgence.[13]

If this argument sounds vaguely familiar, it may be because another author wrote such a treatise centuries ago: the author of the Book of Job in the Hebrew Scriptures. Much of what Christians call the Old Testament reflects the ancient mentality known as retribution theology, which holds that the good prosper and the evil don't. Even though human experience proves over and over again that this is not the case, we humans are reluctant to let go, even today, of what we would consider the way things ought to be. The books of the Old Testament known as the Writings, or Wisdom Literature, deal with retribution theology with varying degrees of skepticism. The Book of Job, in particular, takes clear aim at the shortcomings of this mentality, but the book is long and complex. In fact, as we have it today, Job is apparently a combination of two earlier works, since there is a long prose version bookended by a version in poetry.

Whatever the difficulties in interpreting Job, the effort is worth the struggle, for the Book of Job stands as a primitive handbook for grief counselors: a how-to manual both for how to deal with persons in grief and how *not* to proceed. Since Job's wife and friends were raised to believe in retribution theology, they cannot be convinced that Job has, in fact, done nothing wrong, nothing that would warrant the horrible punishments inflicted by God. Even God doesn't come across too well here, since Job's sufferings seem to be the means God uses to win a bet with Satan.

Eventually, God does hear Job's cries for vindication. God comes and sits with Job and holds forth on the wonders of creation, all of which are beyond Job's ability to plan or create. One scripture scholar has suggested that the important thing is not so much what God says, since the words could easily be heard as a further rebuke of Job; the important thing is the fact that God did hear Job, did listen, did come and sit with him.[14] And, as Lewis himself notes in the Preface to *Essays Presented to Charles Williams,* God's displeasure, in

Williams's view, was not directed at the weak, finally impatient Job, but at "the comforters, the self-appointed advocates on God's side, the people who tried to show that all was well—'the sort of people,' he said, immeasurably dropping his lower jaw and fixing me with his eyes—'the sort of people who wrote books on the Problem of Pain.'"[15]

Some forty years after Lewis published his treatise on pain, Rabbi Harold Kushner took up the same theme in his book *When Bad Things Happen to Good People*.[16] Like Lewis, Kushner had suffered a tremendous personal blow. His son Aaron was diagnosed at the age of three with the incurable condition known as progeria (rapid aging). Aaron died just days after his fourteenth birthday. Kushner remarked that he knew at the time Aaron was diagnosed that he would someday write this book, and he knew after Aaron died that it had to be a book of hope. It had to be a book for both those who wanted to continue believing in God but were also too angry with God to believe, and those who, fearing anger at God, blamed themselves for their own pain.

Much of the harm that is done by well-intentioned believers as they try to help a grieving friend springs from their inability to explain why God would "allow" such things to happen. They feel the need to "defend" God. If we value each individual life and are scandalized at innocent suffering, how can we then be told that this is all "God's plan"?

Kushner, like Lewis, looks at the implications of believing in a God who is both all-good and all-powerful. If both these things are true, then why do good people suffer? Using the Book of Job, Kushner suggests that we are presented with three beliefs:[17]

- God is all-powerful. Nothing happens in the world unless God wills it.
- God is just and fair. (Note the retribution theology.)
- Job is a good person.

All three of these statements work *as long as* Job remains healthy and wealthy. Once Job loses his health and his wealth, then only two of these statements can be true. "The argument of the Book of Job [is] an argument over which of the three statements we are prepared to sacrifice, so that we can keep on believing the other two."[18]

Kushner suggests—and I agree with him—that we can hold B and C and give up A. "Forced to choose between a good God who is not totally powerful, or a powerful God who is not totally good, the author of the book of Job chooses to believe in God's goodness." The image of an all-powerful God brings false comfort, since this is a God who guarantees fair treatment and happy endings. On the other hand, a God who is all-just but not all-powerful may not be able to stop bad things from happening, but can strengthen and console us when they do. The biblical God supports the poor, the widowed, and the orphaned, but they continue to be poor and widowed and orphaned.[19] What we experience as anger at God is, in reality, anger at what we perceive as an unjust situation. Perhaps our compassion comes from God, and God's anger is expressed in our own indignation. Maybe that is what it means to be made in God's image.

Claiming that suffering is "God's will" is both dangerous and arbitrary. Such a claim forces us to jump through mental hoops, to rationalize, to try to explain the unexplainable. Why not just accept random tragedy and see such things as sorrowful and appalling to God, too? Kushner even criticizes the insurance industry's habit of referring to natural disasters as "acts of God." The act of God, he says, is not the disaster but the courageous people who rebuild their lives and the generous people who help them.[20] Suffering people don't need theology; they need sympathy, compassion, and reassurance.

How often has a friend cried out in pain, "Why me?" And how often, in our misguided attempts to comfort him or her, have we answered that question? It is not truly a question, but precisely a cry of pain. Our answers can do a disservice to God or even make the ones suffering feel that they somehow "deserved" the pain they now experience. In an odd way, we humans would rather believe that we deserve our fate than admit that there might be randomness abroad in the land.

Kushner's book is filled with stories that illustrate both the right and the wrong way to help people develop an approach to grief. Among them he notes how often people try to console small children who have lost a parent. Have we ever heard—or said ourselves—"Don't feel bad; God needed your mother more than you did?" In one sentence, in eleven little words, we have made at least three major mistakes: We have denied the child the right to his or her emotions. We have placed the blame squarely on God. And at the same time, we have reserved guilt for the child who didn't need his mother "enough."[21]

The Lewis who wrote *The Problem of Pain* betrayed little if any doubt about the role of suffering in human life. "God whispers to us in our pleasures, speaks in our conscience, but shouts in our pains: it is [God's] megaphone to rouse a deaf world." Pain is what makes us aware of our evil, so it is not the act of a vengeful God. "No doubt Pain as God's megaphone is a terrible instrument; it may lead to final and unrepented rebellion. But it gives the only opportunity the bad [person] can have for amendment. It removes the veil, it plants the flag of truth within the fortress of a rebel soul."[22]

Pain also reminds us that God is in charge. We tend not to turn to God when things are going well. God realizes that even modest prosperity can keep us from perfection. Lewis sees God's troubling of righteous souls as an act of "divine humility," because God "stoops" to conquer us even when we ignore God.[23]

Pain is a test that shatters our self-sufficiency and teaches us that our real strength comes from God and from conformity to God's will. "The real problem is not why some humble, pious, believing people suffer, but why some do not." But pain is still pain, and pain hurts. And, as soon as the crisis has passed, we revert to our former carelessness; this is what necessitates tribulation without ceasing.[24]

All treatises on grief eventually deal with the role of prayer. Why do we pray? Does prayer "work?" In the movie *Shadowlands,* when Lewis is asked by his colleagues whether he continues to pray in the midst of his immense sorrow over Joy's death, he responds that he does. He goes on to explain that God doesn't need his prayers—*he* does. He prays because he cannot not pray. Earlier in the film, one of his students had quoted his schoolteacher-father as saying that we read to know we are not alone. Lewis and Kushner and generations of believers have discovered that the same is true of prayer. Prayer doesn't change God: it changes us. And prayer lets us know that we are not alone, not just because it connects us with God, but also because it connects us to each other. We stand with all the believers who ever lived, who live today, who ever will live, and we borrow their strength to supplement our weakness.

The community of the small Philadelphia college where I teach recently went through a series of astonishing losses. One of our juniors, for example, died in childbirth—yes, in childbirth. Another was burned to death when her car was part of a multi-vehicle accident on the infamous Schuylkill Expressway. The dean's secretary, who had never smoked, was diagnosed with bilateral lung cancer and was dead in a matter of months. A bit later, one of our graduates was murdered, apparently the victim of a random act of violence. Now, any institution must expect to have to deal with the occasional death or tragic accident. In our case, however, the number of losses was disproportionate to our size, and some of those losses were numbing. We did the only thing we could. After months of one wake, one funeral, after another, we gathered in a parlor and prayed and wept and lit candles for our lost loved ones.

Yes, prayer does help. Whether you share a mutual faith tradition, or hold no faith tradition at all, gathering in prayer and remembrance is sometimes the only way through the tunnel of grief. Somehow saying familiar words soothes us, their rhythm washing over our pain, relaxing us, rather like the worry beads Greek fishermen run constantly over their fingers or the rosary beads caressed by elderly widows at early Mass. Praying does not change God; praying usually does not result in any perceptible external changes in us or our world. The suffering continue to suffer, the dead stay dead, the heart still grieves. But prayer unites us to a strength outside ourselves and helps us get through each day a little bit stronger, a little bit more whole, a little closer to reconciliation and restoration.

Lewis's conversion also changed his concept of the afterlife. Before his conversion, Lewis was so pessimistic that he didn't even *want* life to continue after death. Death ended all, and that was just as it should be. And, if the troubles of this world got to be unbearable, suicide was always an option. In *Surprised by Joy,* Lewis went so far as to say that "the horror of the Christian universe was that it had no door marked *Exit*."[25] But even after his conversion, Jack was not convinced of the importance or even the efficacy of belief in an afterlife. He noted Judaism's lack of belief in or concern about life after death. He felt that what came after death, be it happiness or misery, was not, strictly speaking, a religious subject. Various beliefs in the afterlife reflected our own hopes or anxieties. God is God, apart from any such belief. Better to develop a healthy concept of and belief in God first. In Judaism, lack of belief in an afterlife led to concern for prosperity on all levels: individual, communal, and national. Old Testament people cried to God for justice; Christians cry to God for mercy. Lewis felt the older stance was the stronger one.[26]

5

I Shall Never Be a Biped Again

A Discussion of A Grief Observed

Remember
HELEN JOY
DAVIDMAN
D. July 1960
Loved wife of C. S. LEWIS

Here the whole world (stars, water, air,
And field, and forest as they were
Reflected in a single mind)
Like cast-off clothes was left behind
In ashes yet with hope that she,
Re-born from holy poverty,
In *Lenten Lands,* hereafter may
Resume them on her Easter Day.[1]

"No one ever told me that grief felt so like fear."[2] In his preface to the 1994 edition of *A Grief Observed,* Joy's son Douglas Gresham writes that the book "is a stark recounting of one man's studied attempts to come to grips with and in the end defeat the emotional paralysis of the most shattering grief of his life" (6).

In his own autobiographical work, *Lenten Lands,* Gresham describes *A Grief Observed* as a book that is simply true, without padding:

> It is the simple and literal description of Jack's own feelings and his intellectual and logical reactions to those crushing emotional hammer blows. Jack did not pad; the very essence of his writing style is its simplicity and shining clarity. He did not obscure or bend the truth to make it more acceptable; that would have been contrary to his nature.[3]

Nicholi makes this observation: Where *The Problem of Pain* was "a cerebral work dealing with the intellectual aspects of the problem," *A Grief Observed* is "a more emotional, visceral response to the death of his wife."[4] Robert Morneau agrees that *A Grief Observed* is intensely personal, while *The Problem of Pain* is abstract and highly impersonal. In the earlier book, Lewis is a somewhat distant observer, while in *A Grief Observed* he is a participant. Morneau goes on to say that faith, after all, "is more a matter of experience than of logical content."[5]

Christopher Mitchell, however, disagrees that the two books are so very different. Once Lewis began to emerge from the worst of his grief, Mitchell claims, he went back to the same principles he had set forth in the earlier book. "He expressed them differently, and I think he had a deeper understanding of those principles than he had before, but he didn't overthrow those things. Those ideas were the things he fell back on. The temptations he dealt with in *A Grief Observed* were approached or dealt with to some extent in *The Problem of Pain.*"[6]

C. S. Lewis and Human Suffering

C. S. Lewis and Joy Davidman were, as we have seen, both writers, both academically talented, both later-in-life committed Christians. In Joy, Jack found, much to his delight and amazement, an intellectual equal. In all other aspects of their lives and personalities they could not have been more different. He was a bachelor don in the most prestigious halls of British academia, she an outspoken American poet. Jack was middle class, Irish and English, and filled with concepts of personal honor, good manners, and chivalry. Joy was lower-middle class, born Jewish of second-generation Ukrainian and Polish immigrants from the Bronx. Jack and Joy found each other and became friends, spouses, and then lovers who adored each other: this may sound nearly too good to be true, a Hollywood fantasy, but that is precisely what happened.[7] In fact, *A Grief Observed* would seem to answer those Lewis fans who still find it difficult to accept his relationship with Joy as one of true, deeply human love. Without this woman, who had become his "other half," the completion of him, Lewis felt diminished. "Having found in her the reality which he had always sought, he now faces the possibility of that reality fading into an unreal artifice of his own making."[8]

The fantasy ended much too quickly, however, and most of their time together was a mixture of extreme happiness and deep sadness. Jack responded to Joy's suffering and death in the only way he knew: he wrote a journal that appeared soon after its completion as *A Grief Observed*. Jack himself had never planned to publish his thoughts. When he showed it to his literary agent, Spencer Curtis Brown, he used the name *Dimidius* (Latin for "halved"). Walter Hooper finds this "a revealing statement of the unity of two people which [Lewis's] marriage had meant to him."[9] T. S. Eliot, at the time a director of the publishing company, recognized the work as Lewis's and suggested the author use a "more plausible" English pen name, so the first edition was published under a pseudonym, N. W. Clerk.[10] It is a book of stark honesty and unadorned simplicity, describing, as Douglas Gresham put, "a man emotionally naked in his own Gethsemane...The book has a power which is rare,...the power of unabashed truth" (11–12).

Lewis's journals describe the nightmare journey faced by anyone who has lost a loved one. Lewis came to realize that grief is complex and overwhelming, something which no one else can truly share. You want and need other people around you and yet you have no interest in them. Lewis referred to Joy as "H"; he feared he would lose the memory of the real person.

Lewis found that there is a "laziness" to grief. Except for his job, any effort was too much. He likened himself to a "dog-tired man who wants an extra blanket on a cold night; [yet] he'd rather lie there shivering than get up and find one" (12).

In the 1950s, Lewis had published *Mere Christianity*. In that work, he had dealt with pain and suffering from the vantage point of one who has all the answers: God will make us perfect, no matter how much the process causes us to suffer. Our suffering is like the blows of the chisel as the Divine Sculptor shapes us into our perfect selves.[11] Joy's illness and death challenged those smug assumptions. Now God seemed to slam the door in Lewis's face. Why, Jack wondered, was God present in the good times but absent in the bad? The danger, moreover, was not so much that he would not believe in God, but that he would believe such dreadful things about God (22–23).

Jack felt like an embarrassment to everyone else. His friends and colleagues couldn't decide whether or not to bring "it" up. In Jack's case, this was all made more complicated by the fact that many in his inner circle had never truly accepted Joy from the beginning. She represented such a dramatic departure from normalcy as they understood it that they simply ignored her existence. Now they had no idea how to handle their anguished friend. Jack saw, too, the fear in the faces of other couples. "Perhaps the bereaved ought to be isolated in special settlements like lepers" (27).

Lewis mused on the idea of cancer. He decided that there really is no such thing as cancer; there are accumulated ups and downs, good moments and bad moments, and, although he did his best to share Joy's journey, in the end they each had their own experience. "I had my miseries, not hers; she had hers, not mine. The end of hers would be the coming-of-age of mine. We were setting out on different roads. This cold truth, this terrible traffic-regulation ('You, Madam, to the right—you, Sir, to the left') is just the beginning of the separation which is death itself" (30).

Jack discovered he had little patience for euphemisms. Death is death. As the days went by, Joy's face became a blur but her voice lingered and could turn Jack "at any moment to a whimpering child" (32). As the weeks passed, Jack realized he could feel "the slow, insidious beginning of a process" that would make Joy less real and more the product of his imagination. He felt the need for the real Joy who had changed his life, and said about himself, "Oh God, God, why did you take such trouble to force this creature out of its shell if it is now doomed to crawl back—to be sucked back—into it?" (34–35).

Although Jack could pray for the "other dead," he could not bring himself to pray for Joy. "You never know how much you really believe anything until its truth or falsehood becomes a matter of life and death to you" (38–39). He also had difficulty interpreting well-meant phrases like "She is with God" or "She is at peace." What did they mean? Where was Joy, if she still existed? (43–44) "Why should the separation...which so agonizes the lover who is left behind be painless to the lover who departs?" And, if Joy was in God's hands, well, she was all along, wasn't she? And anyway, Jack lamented, he had seen what those hands did to her (41). "Talk to me about the truth of religion and I'll listen gladly. Talk to me about the duty of religion and I'll listen submissively. But don't come talking to me about the consolation of religion or I shall suspect that you don't understand." Jack began to see God as a divine vivisector who

52

baited even Christ on the cross. It took a long time for him to view all these images as too anthropomorphic, too earthbound (38–46).[12]

Perhaps the best we can do with suffering is to suffer it. "Will there come a time when I no longer ask why the world is like a mean street, because I shall take the squalor as normal? Does grief finally subside into boredom tinged by faint nausea?" (53). Rationally, we know that suffering is to be expected; it's part of the bargain that is life. But this is suffering in the abstract, suffering that happens to somebody else. Does that mean that what had passed as faith was mere imagination? If a house of cards can be knocked down so fast, then perhaps it is a good thing that suffering came along and showed it for what it was.

Striking out at God brings momentary relief. It is easier to see God as a veterinarian and not a vivisector in our own suffering than in that of someone we love. And yet Lewis came to understand that wanting Joy back would also be selfish, since she would one day have to die all over again. His grief was intermittent; her pain was unrelenting. In several places in his writing, Lewis reflected on the difficulties Lazarus might have experienced after Jesus called him back from the dead. And of those who claim to have no fear of God, because God is good, Lewis asked, "Have they never been to a dentist?" (50–61).

At one point Lewis likened grief to suspense. So many habitual actions no longer have a target. Yet, it was precisely when he began a tentative recovery that he could once again feel Joy and remember her more clearly. When friends told him that what he and Joy had was "too perfect to last," Jack's first response was that, if their comment were true, then what a sadist God must be, looking down and saying, Aha! You're too happy. But, he discovered, the interpretation could be that he and Joy had got that lesson right and it was time to move on. Bereavement "follows marriage as normally as marriage follows courtship or as autumn follows summer.

C. S. Lewis and Human Suffering

It is not a truncation of the process but one of its phases; not the interruption of the dance, but the next figure" (66–68).

As the healing process began, Lewis likened "getting over" the loved one's death to recovering from the amputation of a leg. Nothing is ever the same. "At present I am learning to get about on crutches. Perhaps I shall presently be given a wooden leg. But I shall never be a biped again" (71). There is, too, a sort of shame in feeling better. If we don't hurt, are we killing the dead a second time? Having been joined into one flesh, we are no longer whole. But too much emphasis on mourning may actually keep the loved one at a greater distance. "I will turn to her as often as possible in gladness. I will even salute her with a laugh. The less I mourn her the nearer I seem to her" (74). Even such optimistic thoughts, though, cannot hold the black moods completely at bay. The phases of grief and recovery are cyclical. "Am I going in circles, or dare I hope I am on a spiral?" (75). Grief often seems fresh, the wound new.

Writing the journal helped Jack personally, but the exercise failed to accomplish another goal: it could not explain sorrow. Lewis thought he could describe the "state" of sorrow, make a map of the territory. "Sorrow, however, turns out to be not a state but a process. It needs not a map but a history....Grief is like a long valley where any bend may reveal a totally new landscape" (75, 77).

Lewis realized that he could now go back to his former haunts and actually find some pleasure in them. But that, too, was both daunting and troublesome: did his love and marriage mean nothing? "Did you ever know, my dear, how much you took away with you when you left? You have stripped me even of my past, even of the things we never shared" (77–78).

Healing comes slowly, but it does come. Unlike a sudden transition, Lewis likened it to "the warming of a room or the coming of daylight. When you first notice them they have already been going on for some time" (79).

I Shall Never Be a Biped Again

So, through this little book, this slender volume of love, loss, pain, grief, and healing, Lewis summoned those who grieve to grieve honestly; only then can they find hope in the midst of sorrow. We must, he insisted, admit our doubts, vent our angers, acknowledge our fears. Then our hearts will have room for the healing balm of grace and love.

6

An Approach to Mourning

Our Own "Grief Observed"

I also have become much acquainted with grief now through the death of my great friend Charles Williams, my friend of friends, the comforter of all our little set, the most angelic man. The odd thing is that his death has made my faith stronger than it was a week ago. And I find that all the talk about "feeling that he is closer to us than before" isn't just talk. It's just what it does feel like—I can't put it into words. One seems at moments to be living in a new world. Lots, lots of pain, but not a particle of depression or resentment.[1]

People whose faith is grounded in the Bible can start their reflection on the true meaning of grief by reviewing what the Bible and recent theologians have to say about suffering and death as part of the human condition. The Christian understanding of death is not concerned simply with clinical definitions, although they are important. Theology sees death as the final point of the human person's individual history.

An Approach to Mourning

In the Old Testament, death is considered a normal event to be expected after a long and full life. The fate of the deceased is expressed in terms of *sheol*, a dark, cheerless realm of the dead where there is no happiness or praise of God. Wisdom Literature, as we have seen already in the Book of Job, includes significant reflection on death. Later, under the influence of Greek philosophy, the notion of an immortal soul introduces the belief that the just ones who die are in the hands of God. Eventually, there developed hope for some sort of meaningful survival after death and a concept of resurrection.

The Christian addition to the bible, the New Testament or Christian Scriptures, adds reflection on the redemptive meaning of Christ's death. Jesus is vindicated by his resurrection; through the power of his death and resurrection, Jesus overcomes the power of death. Paul assures Christians that, just as Christ died and was raised, so those who believe in him will also be raised to eternal life.

More recent Christian theology has tried to relate death to the mystery of sin and redemption, but it is inadequate to see suffering merely as a punishment for sin, or to see death only as the separation of body and soul. As the final moment of a free, personal history, death is seen as the decisive act of human freedom in which the person can either accept or reject the mystery of God and thereby put the final seal on his or her history and destiny.

Many contemporary theologians have moved away from any notion of death as the direct result of sin. Since biblical scholarship has opened up Genesis in new ways, and many Christians have espoused a historical-critical reading of scripture, there is no need to "justify" God's condemnation of all humans because of the poor choice of one unfortunate—and very young, very naive—couple. Karl Rahner, for example, has observed that it is not the fact of death that is the result of sin, but the way we feel about death, seeing it as darkness and a threat. Rahner saw the central mystery of death as the free act by which we give ourselves over into the hands of God's love and mercy; this is the way believers enter fully into the dying of Christ.

So, the basic mystery of death can be anticipated throughout our lives in the "little dying" by which we give ourselves over to God and others through works of charity. The moment of death itself is the ultimate act of human freedom.

Moral theologians who discuss life as a series of moral choices speak of a "fundamental option"; that is, our basic stance toward God. If our disposition toward the presence of God in our lives is one of openness and acceptance, then our "final option" at the moment of death will ratify that choice and unite us to God for all eternity. Hell, then, is not an external punishment imposed by a wrathful God, but the final choice of a person who consistently rebelled against God and chose selfish autonomy throughout life. It seems to me that, were he alive today, Lewis would see the beauty of this approach. Hell is not found directly in scripture. Yet our contemporary image of hell makes us aware of the seriousness of human choices. Human freedom must include the possibility of the definitive rejection of God.

Just as the Hebrews wanted retribution theology to operate without exception so too some Christians find comfort in denying the possibility of hell. Universalists, as they are sometimes called, insist that in the end God's love will triumph and not a single soul will be lost. As attractive as this theory is—and remember, no one knows for sure—its one great flaw is its failure to take human freedom seriously. Human life is about choices, choices that are made freely and with knowledge about their consequences. We believe that God freely accepted self-limitation in order to endow us with free will. God's respect for free will must be absolute or it is a meaningless gift. And, if we are free to accept God, then we must likewise be free to reject that same God. This insistence on free will can be found in many of Lewis's works.

An Approach to Mourning

What does eternal life mean? Eternal life is a participation in the life of God, which begins in the present and comes to fullness after death. It is not just unending existence, which even those who choose against God will have, but a personal relationship with God through the Holy Spirit. It is the future perfection of the personal knowledge of God that was begun in faith.

Christian theology traditionally speaks of the "final things." Eschatology is the study of the final state of the universe, the goal toward which God is moving all creation. It is becoming ever clearer, however, that too much emphasis on what awaits beyond the grave can deafen us to the needs of the here and now. Better to concentrate on the present, since it is out of the present that the future will emerge. Here, too, I hear echoes of Lewis's thought.

A holistic approach to grief, then, will assure those who mourn that we have faith in life everlasting, but will also attend to their needs today. Christians can learn from their Jewish brothers and sisters, who are more concerned with human needs at the time of sorrow and whose rituals are imbued with a deep understanding of the human psyche. Recall, for example, their covering of mirrors in a house of mourning. This simple gesture assures those within that how they "look" during these first hard days is inconsequential.

The earliest Christians reached out to the sick and dying by visiting them and anointing them with oil, an ancient symbol of strength and healing (see Jas 5:14). Catholic churches today still use the oil of the sick. The oil is blessed during the celebration of the chrism Mass on Holy Thursday; the Rite of Blessing says: "Make this oil a remedy for all who are anointed with it; heal them in body, in soul and in spirit, and deliver them from every affliction." The bread of the Eucharist is also shared with the dying person as *viaticum*, "food for the journey"—a beautiful image of the Eucharist as "provisions" for the final journey from life through death to everlasting life. As with Judaism's custom of covering mirrors after a loved one's death, elements of this Catholic ritual may be adapted to bring great meaning and comfort beforehand.[2]

The belief in eternal life leads to one of the most comforting of all Christian concepts; namely, the Communion of Saints. Our faith assures us that all the dead who died in Christ are with God forever. In a very real way, when we participate in the Eucharist or other liturgical rituals, we are in the company of all the generations that went before us. All those who have loved God in the past are united with those of us who are still struggling to live out that love. We can tap into their strength and their example, and we can take comfort from our belief that those people—who were so special to us while they lived, whose example and advice helped make us the persons we have become—are among their number.

All of this flies in the face of contemporary American society, which is to a great extent marked by a denial of suffering of any kind, and in particular, marked by a denial of aging and death. Even though the mystery of death is the central question of human experience, many Americans simply ignore the whole topic. If an approach to grief is to be effective at all, it must begin with an honest acceptance of our own mortality.

Sociologists talk about the changing demographics of death, from the customary at-home deaths of earlier centuries to today's mostly antiseptic, detached hospital deaths. Americans enjoy an ever-increasing life expectancy and a decreasing rate of infant mortality, while our families have gotten smaller and more mobile. Modern medicine and technology seemingly make daily advances, and the whole spectrum of issues surrounding pain, suffering, death, and grief has been turned over to the professionals. Even the causes of death have changed. Where once most adults died of acute diseases, today many older people succumb only after long battles with chronic illness.

Language itself has been manipulated to help us deny the reality of death and grief. Our loved ones "pass" or "leave us" instead of dying, and then they are "interred" or "laid to rest" instead of being buried. Undertakers have evolved into funeral directors.

An honest approach to grief will choose the road not usually taken in American society and call grief by its own name. An honest approach will lament the death of loved ones while recalling the joy of their lives. It will sorrow with those struck by illness or accident, while helping them use to the fullest whatever of their body remains whole. And it will focus on life on earth so that the kingdom of God may become more and more truly present here and now, as we await its glorious fulfillment at the end of time.

So, what do we actually say to those who grieve?

However socially adept we may be, most of us feel unprepared to deal with a friend who's recently lost a parent, spouse, sibling or child. We sincerely want to offer comfort and support, but are unsure of how to go about it. So often, we wind up settling solely for commercial expressions of sympathy in store-bought cards—or...doing nothing at all. Which is sad, because there are such simple ways to lighten a grieving friend's burden.[3]

Those of us who choose to take the road less traveled in our approach to grief still face dilemmas such as those described in the above quotation. It takes a long time and hours of reflection and meditation to come to the realization that there are no answers, at least no human answers, and to be comfortable with that. Like God who sat beside Job without directly answering any of the poor man's questions, we must learn to "companion" our friends, our relatives, and ourselves on the journey of inner healing. The Latin roots of *companion* mean, literally, "to share bread with." In grief, we share the bread of sorrow; in faith, we share the bread of life. Bread is such an important symbol in this emerging spirituality of grief.

Perhaps that image of bread, then, can be used to give us an initial example of a concrete way to be with those who grieve: we can eat with them. We can prepare meals, we can take them out to a special restaurant, we can bring along one of their favorite snacks when we visit. This food-sharing serves more than one purpose; for at a very basic level people in grief often forget to eat or have no interest in eating. But their getting sick will not help their loved one who has died or who is hospitalized or otherwise suffering. By making it both easy and acceptable for the grieving person to eat, to take in nourishment, we are feeding both body and spirit.

To those of us who fear that we don't know what to say, or that we will say the wrong thing, an honest approach to grief replies that anything you say will be "wrong" and everything you say will be "right." In fact, what you say or whether you say anything is not nearly as important as your presence. As I have grown older and espoused this road through grief more and more as my own, I have found myself simply telling my friend that I don't know what to say. There is something amazingly comforting in that admission. It lets both of us off the hook of over-theologizing that which is beyond human comprehension. It lets God off the hook, too, for it leaves me free to observe that life isn't fair and the situation, quite frankly, stinks. We can go on from there, because that is an open-ended acknowledgment both of human limitations and of the possibility of healing. If God is suspect, so is eternity; but if it is the situation that is causing my anxiety, there is still hope of eternal peace.

Remember the remark that we read to know we are not alone and that its extension includes praying to know we are not alone? Well, we grieve with others to let them know they are not alone. That is perhaps the greatest single thing we can do for them. Store-bought cards are not necessarily so bad, provided we add a personal message before we sign our name. My precious Dad died over forty-five years ago, but I still have the folder filled with the many cards and notes Mom received. They still bring tears to my eyes, and they still fill me with gratitude that Dad was appreciated and missed.

In the case of death, sharing a special memory of the loved one who has died can bring a smile to a weary heart. In the case of illness or accident, I have often gone to the hospital armed with a load of coloring books and crayons to amuse and distract the child within the wounded adult in the bed. But I have also learned to leave my platitudes at home, where they will not be allowed to trivialize loss or gloss over sorrow.

There are pamphlets, articles, and books galore that give helpful hints for dealing with grieving people. Mostly they can be distilled into this ancient bit of advice: be yourself. While it is helpful and even necessary to read about the psychology of loss and the effects of grief, my grieving friends are not the subject of a sociological survey. They are hurting human beings and they need me to touch their hearts, not their intellects. It is not my place to tell them how to feel, how long to grieve, or why it isn't really as bad as it seems. Nor do I need to have all the answers, least of all answers about the role of God in this particular loss. A simple "I don't know, either" is worth all the theology at our command.

Bereavement, which literally means "being torn apart," is natural, and it must be an integral part of our understanding of life. Bereavement itself is a complex experience; it includes grief, the internal feeling of loss, and mourning—the public display of that grief through various rituals.[4]

This might be a good place to remind ourselves that this approach to grief applies to us even when, perhaps especially when, we are the ones facing suffering or loss. We humans can get quite adept at dealing with other people and their problems and yet never give ourselves the same consideration. It is not by accident that Jesus' second great commandment directs us to love our neighbors "as ourselves." We must be willing to acknowledge our grief and to accept its effects in our own lives. Major decisions would best be put off until our minds and bodies have had time to heal. Extra rest is not a luxury at such a time, but a real necessity.

Even before his own experience of grief over Joy's death, Lewis seemed to have been aware of the danger that those in mourning might not take care of their own needs. In a letter to his friend Sheldon Vanauken, whose own beloved wife Davy was dying, Lewis wrote: "Be careful of your bodily health. You must be, physically, v. tired, much more tired than you know. Above all, don't yield to the feeling that such things 'don't matter *now*.' You must remain, as she wishes, a good *instrument* for all heavenly impulses to work on, and the body is part of the instrument."[5]

However independent we have prided ourselves on being, a time of grief cries out for support from family, friends, and colleagues. Most of all, we must be willing to go with the flow of our own emotions, erratic as they might be. Let the tears come, at private moments or in the middle of a business meeting. Admit to the down times, no matter what triggers them—and marvel at the diversity and unpredictability of those triggers. Try to find something to help you express your grief. Like C. S. Lewis, you might find a journal helps. Write your own *A Grief Observed*. Seek counseling if it will help you, but don't feel you must if it won't. Exercise, read, eat nutritional meals. In short, do for yourself what you would do for a friend.

Just as we must not put a time limit on our friend's grief, so we must not put such a limit on our outreach to him or her. The passage of time helps in some ways, but also brings with it anniversaries, holidays, birthdays, and other special occasions that can trigger a fresh feeling of helplessness.[6] An unexpected phone call, a holiday invitation, an offer to drive the children to school—any of these gestures can make a difference in a person's ongoing process of healing. Since my mother's death, a particular friend has called before Easter, the Fourth of July, Thanksgiving, and Christmas to find out what my plans are. She is determined that I have the option of being part of her family on those days, if that is what I want and need. Asking honestly how a friend wants to be treated on a certain occasion gives that person the option of asking for company or saying that he or she would rather be alone.

This "road not taken" approach to grief frees us to ask the honest questions, to express the honest emotions, and to give those in grief the room to do the same. That may just be grief's greatest blessing.

7

Only the Life I've Led

Some Concluding Remarks

Lewis was an active, energetic man who looked like a
farmer but talked like a philosopher, who would as soon
lolligag in fairydom as joust in intellectual lists, who rel-
ished the love of friendship, was surprised by the love of
a woman, and cultivated the love of God. He was also a
funny man.[1]

Like many Americans, I had heard of C. S. Lewis over the years,
mainly in connection with the Narnia stories. Once I became a theologian and began teaching on the college level, however, it became
apparent that Lewis had a little gem of a book for nearly every course
I created: *Mere Christianity* for Christian Humanism; *The Screwtape
Letters* for Sacramental Theology; *The Great Divorce* for Roman
Catholicism; and, of course, *A Grief Observed* for Death and Dying. It
also soon became clear to me that, far from being dated, this mid-
twentieth-century Irish don from Oxford University was surprisingly
relevant, his arguments as crisp and concise as they were when he first
wrote them down or spoke them to his many and various audiences.

It also became clear that, like any public figure who captures
the imagination of thousands of readers, Lewis himself is in danger

of being lost in the works he left behind. So I tried to find the "real" Jack, which, I realize, would have made him incredibly angry. Lewis was a literary critic who disdained those who sought the author behind the work. Today's "reality television" would send him over the edge, no doubt.

Owen Barfield, a member of the Inklings and one of Jack's good friends, had this to say:

> As to his growing reputation and the fact that he was quickly becoming a well-known public figure—let me record for the sheer pleasure of it that throughout the whole of his life I never recall a single remark, a single word or silence, a single look, the lightest flicker of an eyelid or hemi-demi-semitone of alteration in the pitch of his voice which would go to suggest that he felt his opinion entitled to more respect than that of old friends he was talking with because, unlike theirs, it had won the ear of tens or hundreds of thousands wherever the English language is spoken and in a good many places where it is not. I wonder how many famous men there have been of whom this could truthfully be said.[2]

Since much of my work is in the area of courses, talks, and workshops on issues connected with death and bereavement, I was particularly struck by the evolution of Lewis's understanding of the role of suffering and death in human life. While it should not have been any great revelation—all of us humans, if we live long enough, grow and develop and change—Lewis emerged for me as an ordinary human being, albeit one extraordinarily talented and productive. He began to deal with suffering and death at an early age, using whatever resources were available to him, and arrived at different conclusions at different points in his life and career.

C. S. Lewis and Human Suffering

Born into a nominally Christian family, young Jack had, I suppose, a fairly conventional image of who God was and what God did. But the death of his mother when he was nine, a death he had prayed to God to stop, tarnished that conventional image. Oh, God probably existed, but now Jack saw a distant, deaf God. The boy's solution? He became a self-styled atheist. And rather nasty experiences in a succession of schools did nothing to redeem God or to bring back Jack's childhood security. Then Jack was sent to France in World War I and saw horrors to last a lifetime.

From 1950 until shortly before his death in 1963, Jack kept up a correspondence with "an American lady," whose identity is unknown to this day. (The letters are addressed to "Dear Mary.") Writing to her in March of 1963, obviously knowing his own end was near and apparently thinking back to his days in the trenches, Jack sympathizes with Mary, who is also quite ill:

> I am sorry they threaten you with a painful disease. "Dangerous" matters much less, doesn't it? What have you and I got to do but make our exit? When they told me I was in danger several months ago, I don't remember feeling distressed. I am talking, of course, about *dying*, not about *being killed*. If shells started falling about this house I should feel quite differently. An external, visible, and (still worse) audible threat at once wakes the instinct of self-preservation into fierce activity. I don't think natural death has any similar terrors.[3]

Jack the atheist doesn't seem to have had any trouble explaining suffering and death: Life is life. Life is hard. Life is full of random and often cruel twists and turns. Without the "out" of a God to blame, this Jack simply took the reality of suffering as a given, even while admitting that suffering still hurts and loss still brings tears.

In midlife, after a lengthy experience of conversion—first to a real belief in God and later to the God of Christianity and to Jesus Christ as the Son of God—Jack put just as much energy into his newly rediscovered faith as he had into his atheism. The literary critic became the lay theologian, popularizing doctrines in lectures, radio broadcasts, and dozens of essays and books. And this was no halfway approach to belief. Jack the convert knew what God wanted and why God allowed us to suffer and to experience loss: Suffering was God's megaphone to rouse us from our deafness, God's chisel to perfect our form. God is good but not indulgent. Bear up, and prepare yourself for later glory.

Then Joy Davidman entered Jack's life. However their relationship began, and whatever Joy's motives in moving to England and becoming increasingly inserted into Jack's life, the fact is that theirs became, for that "one brief, shining moment" that the song from "Camelot" laments, one of the great partnerships and love affairs of the twentieth century. But the cancer that finally forced Jack to admit his growing love for Joy also doomed them to a marriage that ended much too soon.

This Jack now had the experience to go with the theory of his earlier works of Christian apology. The loss of Joy challenged his words about God's use of suffering and sorrow, perhaps even challenged his faith. *This* Jack did what he had done for most of his life: he wrote about it, honestly and starkly, and in so doing, left us one of the best companions any grieving person could ask for on the journey to restoration, the small but powerful journal, *A Grief Observed*.

In talking about Jack's many years as a don at Oxford, his longtime friend George Sayer had this to say:

Although the real man was hidden behind the mask of the self-assured, hearty, argumentative tutor, all of his students shared certain impressions. He was known as a man of exceptional intellectual and even physical vitality, a quality that grew over the years. His flow of wit, humor, and vivid stories told in his deep, rich voice was inexhaustible. He was a good listener as well, and one knew that he would never disclose a confidence entrusted to him. He was a man of his word, a man of integrity, a man of honor.[4]

Jack hated being considered a "popular" writer but seemed to enjoy the success that it brought.[5] Michael White discusses other contradictions he finds in the extraordinary man whose life he chronicled. Jack was not naturally comfortable around women and yet he loved Joy deeply and accepted her as an intellectual equal. He considered having "fans" an absurdity yet tried to reply to every letter he received from them. He never had children of his own and lived in a world of educated adults, yet he is perhaps best known for his Narnia tales. And he seemed to mind many things about academia, yet could never bear the thought of leaving it.[6]

Perhaps it is fitting to leave the last word to Austin Farrer, the close friend and Oxford colleague to whom Jack dedicated his book on the psalms: "The life which Lewis lived with zest he surrendered with composure. He was put almost beside himself by his wife's death; he seemed easy at the approach of his own. He died at the last in a minute. May he everlastingly rejoice in the Mercy he sincerely trusted."[7]

Notes

Preface

1. This warning against just such an endeavor as this book comes from a letter written by J. R. R. Tolkien to Andrew Barrett. Tolkien was lamenting an article about Lewis, written by a former pupil a year after his death. *Letters of J. R. R. Tolkien* (Houghton Mifflin Co., 1964), No. 261. Quoted in George Watson, ed., *Critical Essays on C. S. Lewis* (Aldershot, UK: Scolar Press, 1992), 9.

2. According to one author, the list would include forty books originally handwritten by Lewis, some twenty posthumous collections of his essays, poems, and letters, and over one hundred books about him, including at least four major biographies. See David C. Downing, *The Most Reluctant Convert: C. S. Lewis's Journey to Faith* (Downers Grove, IL: InterVarsity Press, 2002), 12–13.

3. Michael White, *C. S. Lewis: Creator of Narnia* (New York: Carroll & Graf Publishers, 2005), 220.

4. George Sayer, *Jack: A Life of C. S. Lewis* (Wheaton, IL: Crossway Books, 1988), 261.

Introduction: All My Road Before Me

1. Catherine Lynskey Chisham, "The Adventures of Aslan," *Notre Dame Magazine* (Winter 1996–97), 32.

2. Cal Thomas, "C. S. Lewis: The Greatest Mind in Oxford History," *The Intelligencer Record* (July 26, 1998), E2.

3. Brian Sibley, *C. S. Lewis Through the Shadowlands: The Story of His Life with Joy Davidman* (Grand Rapids, MI: Fleming H. Revell, 1994), 22. Sibley is the source of much of this chapter.

4. Donald E. Glover, *C. S. Lewis: The Art of Enchantment* (Athens, OH: Ohio University Press, 1981), 8.

5. Information about Lewis is abundant. One of my sources here is John Boudreau, "Writer Still Speaks to the Soul," *The Philadelphia Inquirer* (November 29, 1998), H5.

6. James T. Como, ed., *C. S. Lewis at the Breakfast Table and Other Reminiscences,* rev. ed. (Orlando, FL: Harcourt Brace Jovanovich, Publishers, 1992), xxi.

7. A. Clifford Morris, *Miles and Miles: Some Reminiscences of an Oxford Taxi Driver and Private Car Hire Service Chauffeur* (Berkshire, Abingdon: The Abbey Press, 1964), 51.

8. Luke Rigby, "A Solid Man," in Como, 39.

9. See Walter Hooper, ed., *All My Road Before Me: The Diary of C. S. Lewis 1922–1927* (New York: Harcourt Brace Jovanovich, 1991).

10. Jocelyn Gibb, ed., *Light on C. S. Lewis* (New York: Harcourt Brace Jovanovich, 1965), vi–vii.

11. Kathleen Raine, "From a Poet," quoted in Gibb, 102–5.

12. Morris, 51.

13. Morris, 53.

14. Glover, 1, 28.

15. Ibid., 3.

16. *New York Times*, November 25, 1963.

17. C. S. Lewis, *The Great Divorce* (New York: MacMillan Publishing Company, 1946), 5–6.

18. From *Dymer,* Part I, quoted in Hooper, *All My Road,* 9.

Notes

1. Bits of a Life

1. Michael White, *C. S. Lewis: Creator of Narnia* (New York: Carroll & Graff Publishers, 2005), x–xi. Neville Coghill, an Oxford don and friend of Lewis, once described that voice as having "the taste of noble wine." See Neville Coghill, "The Approach to English," in Jocelyn Gibb, ed., *Light on C. S. Lewis* (New York: Harcourt Brace Jovanovich, 1965), 54.

2. It is difficult to know what to include of Lewis's life in a book like this. So many biographies of the man already exist. In fact, one of the latest was published in 2005 by Lewis's stepson Douglas Gresham, because so many others were written by people who never knew Jack. See Douglas Gresham, *Jack's Life: The Life Story of C. S. Lewis* (Nashville, TN: Broadman & Holman Publishers, 2005).

3. John Lawlor, *C. S. Lewis: Memories and Reflections* (Dallas, TX: Spence, 1999), 67.

4. David Downing considers this incident highly revealing: despite others' expectations, Lewis "would spend the rest of his life defining himself, and his world, differently from the conventions he had inherited." See David C. Downing, *The Most Reluctant Convert: C. S. Lewis's Journey to Faith* (Downers Grove, IL: InterVarsity Press, 2002), 19.

5. C. S. Lewis, *Surprised by Joy: The Shape of My Early Life* (San Diego: Harcourt Brace & Company, 1955), 10. In an interesting note, Lewis claims that an inherited defect—only one functional joint in the thumb—drove him to writing. Lewis, *Joy,* 12.

6. Downing, 24. Lewis himself is said to have had quite a temper. See, for example, Armand M. Nicholi, *The Question of God: C. S. Lewis and Sigmund Freud Debate God, Love, Sex, and the Meaning of Life* (New York: The Free Press, 2002), 153: "Lewis apparently had a temper he found difficult to control."

7. Nicholi, 26–27.

8. White, 15.

9. Downing, 25–26. Downing goes on to describe Lewis's "boyhood" as oppressive, marked by intellectual languor, the cessation of *joy,* and the pursuit of more prosaic pleasures. He notes that even the clothes changed, from comfortable play-clothes to an itchy uniform (35).

10. White, 16–18.

11. Nicholi, 28.

12. White, 19–20.

13. Ibid., 22.

14. Ibid., 21.

15. Ibid., 30–31.

16. Cited in Walter Hooper, ed., *They Stand Together: The Letters of C. S. Lewis to Arthur Greeves (1914–1963)* (New York: Macmillan Publishing Co., Inc., 1979), 25. Hooper feels that Lewis's letters to Greeves, which continued until shortly before Lewis's death in 1963, "may be as close as we shall ever get to Lewis himself." Hooper, 12.

17. White, 39.

18. Lewis, *Joy,* 17–18.

19. Ibid., 72–77.

20. Downing, 44. For a full description of life at Wynyard, see 36–44.

21. Lewis, *Joy,* 60, 66.

22. Downing, 49.

23. Lewis, *Joy,* 115. On the other hand, even while rejecting God, Lewis saw reality in the gods of the classical myths he so enjoyed.

24. White, 13.

25. Downing, 57.

26. Nicholi, 32.

27. White, 104.

28. Coghill, in Gibb, 52.

29. Ibid., 54–55.

30. Downing, 64–66, 156. See also C. S. Lewis, *Selected Literary Essays,* Walter Hooper, ed. (Cambridge: Cambridge University Press, 1966), 265.

31. George Sayer, *Jack: A Life of C. S. Lewis* (Wheaton, IL: Crossway Books, 1988), 115, 118, 125–26. At the time Lewis met Mrs. Moore, she was forty-five and separated from her husband. She lived in Bristol, but had taken rooms in Oxford with Maureen to be near Paddy during his military training. "Lewis seems to have taken a great liking to Mrs. Moore from the first, and even,…to have been youthfully infatuated by her." Hooper, *They Stand,* 199.

32. White, 91–92.

33. Donald E. Glover, *C. S. Lewis: The Art of Enchantment* (Athens, OH: Ohio University Press, 1981), 15–16.

34. Sayer, 152–55. Like the later relationship between Lewis and Joy Davidman, that between Jack and Mrs. Moore has been dissected by nearly every Lewis biographer. As I was reading one of Lewis's early diaries, it struck me that a big part of his attraction to Mrs. Moore and Maureen was simply that they were Irish. See Walter Hooper, ed., *All My Road Before Me: The Diary of C. S. Lewis 1922–1927* (New York: Harcourt Brace Jovanovich, Publishers, 1991), 1.

35. Sayer, 161–62. Mrs. Moore died in 1951.

36. White, 87–89. Tolkien was born in South Africa in 1892; he lost his father when he was four and his mother when he was twelve. In 1925, Tolkien was appointed chair of Anglo-Saxon at Oxford.

37. Sayer, 249–50.

38. Coghill, in Gibb, 65.

39. Sayer, 358–59.

40. The title echoes that of a poem by William Wordsworth: "Surprised by Joy—Impatient as the Wind." See M. H. Abrams,

gen. ed., *William Wordsworth: The Complete Poetical Works* (London: Macmillan and Co., 1888).

41. Sayer, 326–28. Lewis's friend Humphrey Howard remarked that the book could have been titled *Suppressed by Jack*.

42. Lyle W. Dorsett, *A Love Observed: Joy Davidman's Life & Marriage to C. S. Lewis* (Wheaton, IL: Harold Shaw Publishers, 1998), 4–5. On the other hand, Joy had a painfully crooked spine and suffered from Grave's disease, a form of hyperthyroidism, which resulted in bulging eyes. Instead of surgery, Joy went through a year of radiation treatments. Years later, doctors would connect this to her cancer. Dorsett, 12.

43. Ibid., 9.

44. Ibid., xi.

45. Oliver Pilat, "Girl Communist," *New York Post,* October 3–November 13, 1949. Cited in Dorsett, 21.

46. Dorsett, 33.

47. "Letter to a Comrade" was published by Stephen Vincent Benét in the Yale series. As a result, Joy established a relationship with Brandt & Brandt publishers. More significantly, she was also introduced to the MacDowell Colony in New Hampshire, a gathering place for writers. The poem also won the Loines Memorial Fund Award given by the National Institute of Arts and Letters, for 1938–39. She shared the award with Robert Frost. Dorsett, 25, 36.

48. Ibid., 2–3. Joy's mother made "perfunctory nods at Judaism" (p. 2), while her father was an outspoken atheist. The generation before them had been Orthodox. Her mother's family emigrated from the Ukraine and her father's from Poland so that their children could get an education. "Joy actually grew up in a family where religion was at once respected and deplored" (p. 1).

49. Ibid., xi. Bel Kaufman, author of *Up the Down Staircase,* was Joy's best friend at Hunter. Dorsett attributes Joy's decision to

leave teaching at least in part to her "permanent substitute" status, a Depression tactic to save money. Dorsett, 17, 24.

50. See, for example, Joy Davidman, "The Longest Way Round," in David Wesley Soper, ed., *These Found the Way: Thirteen Converts to Protestant Christianity* (Philadelphia: Westminster Press, 1951), 11–26.

51. Ibid., 23.

52. Ibid., 24.

53. Dorsett, xii.

54. Ibid., 90–91, 118–19, 121.

55. White, 181–83.

56. C. S. Lewis, Foreword, in Joy Davidman, *Smoke on the Mountain: An Interpretation of the Ten Commandments* (Philadelphia: The Westminster Press, 1954), 7.

57. Coincidentally, the colleges bear the same names with variant spellings (and they are both pronounced "mawdlin").

58. Brian Sibley, *C. S. Lewis Through the Shadowlands: The Story of His Life with Joy Davidman* (Grand Rapids, MI: Fleming H. Revell, 1994), 119. Lewis's friend Owen Barfield had helped Lewis set up the Agape Fund, the Agapargyry (lover + money); until he married in 1957, Lewis had two-thirds of all royalties from his Christian writings paid into it. The fund distributed gifts anonymously to people in need. He probably funded the boys' schooling through this trust. See Walter Hooper, *C. S. Lewis: Companion & Guide* (San Francisco: Harper San Francisco, 1996), 32.

59. Lewis felt this prohibition did not apply in Joy's case: Bill was already divorced when she married him, so the Church would not have, in fact, considered her married at all.

60. Dorsett, ix–x.

61. Nicholi, 155.

62. Sayer, 373, 375.

2. The Loss of Conviction

1. K. J. Gilchrist, *A Morning after War: C. S. Lewis and WWI* (New York: Peter Lang, 2005), dedication.

2. Thomas Gray, quoted in Arthur Thomas Quiller-Couch, ed., *The Oxford Book of English Verse 1250–1900* (Oxford: Clarendon, 1919), #453.

3. Armand M. Nicholi, *The Question of God: C. S. Lewis and Sigmund Freud Debate God, Love, Sex, and the Meaning of Life* (New York: The Free Press, 2002), 113. See also Donald Glover, *C. S. Lewis: The Art of Enchantment* (Athens, OH: Ohio University Press, 1981), 32–33.

4. C. S. Lewis, Letters to Dom Bede Griffiths, Volume I (1931–1948), #12, the Marion Wade Center Collection, Wheaton College, Wheaton, Illinois.

5. In his autobiography, Lewis recalls that he arrived in the trenches on his nineteenth birthday. He served mostly around Arras, in the villages of Fampoux and Moncy. He was wounded at Mt. Bernenchon, near Lillers, some six months later. See C. S. Lewis, *Surprised by Joy: The Shape of My Early Life* (San Diego: Harcourt Brace & Company, 1955), 188.

6. Michael White, *C. S. Lewis: Creator of Narnia* (New York: Carroll & Graf Publishers, 2005), 42.

7. Paul Fussell, *The Great War and Modern Memory* (Oxford: Oxford University Press, 1975), 40.

8. Gilchrist, 12, 20.

9. Ibid., 91.

10. Ibid., 79, 83, 87.

11. C. S. Lewis, *Collected Letters Volume I: Family Letters 1905–1931* (London: HarperCollins, 2000), 55.

12. Lewis was actually wounded by British shells, a case of "friendly fire." See Walter Hooper, ed., *They Stand Together: The*

Letters of C. S. Lewis to Arthur Greeves (1914–1963) (New York: Macmillan Publishing Co., Inc., 1979), 212.

13. Lewis, *Joy,* 197.

14. James Como, ed., *C. S. Lewis at the Breakfast Table, and Other Reminiscences* (New York: Macmillan, 1979), 5–6.

15. Collected Letters no. 1, 378.

16. George Sayer: *Jack: A Life of C. S. Lewis* (Wheaton, IL: Crossway Books, 1988), 131–33, 139.

17. Hooper, *They Stand Together,* 240.

18. C. S. Lewis, *Spirits in Bondage: A Cycle of Lyrics,* Walter Hooper, ed., (San Diego: Harcourt Brace & Company, 1984).

19. Gilchrist, 5.

20. Sayer, 144.

21. Gilchrist, 137, 140–41, 145.

22. Walter Hooper, ed., *All My Road Before Me: The Diary of C. S. Lewis 1922–1927* (New York: Harcourt Brace Jovanovich, Publishers, 1991), 51.

23. White, 51–52. White notes that Lewis devoted only half a chapter of *Joy* to his war experiences, compared with eleven chapters on his childhood and education.

24. David C. Downing, *The Most Reluctant Convert: C. S. Lewis's Journey to Faith* (Downers Grove, IL: InterVarsity Press, 2002), 83.

25. White, 65. Gilchrist adds: "The war did not fit into the ruthless logic that Lewis was known to wield." See Gilchrist, 175.

26. Walter Hooper, *C. S. Lewis: Companion and Guide* (San Francisco: Harper San Francisco, 1996), 141.

27. Ibid. John Duncan points out that Lewis's book *The Problem of Pain,* published in 1940, was commissioned during World War II by the Christian Challenge series, and reflects Lewis's approach to the question of how a God who is both good and powerful could allow people to suffer such disaster. See John

Ryan Duncan, *The Magic Never Ends: The Life and Works of C. S. Lewis* (Nashville, TN: W Publishing Group, 2001), 76.

28. Gilchrist, 175–76; Hooper, *Collected Letters,* 422.

29. Gilchrist, 184.

30. Ibid., 188, 190.

31. Ibid., 196.

32. Ibid., 204, 215.

33. C. S. Lewis, *A Grief Observed* (New York: HarperCollins Publishers, 1994), 58.

34. Hooper, *Collected Letters,* 320.

3. Conviction Rediscovered

1. C. S. Lewis, *Surprised by Joy: The Shape of My Early Life* (San Diego: Harcourt Brace & Company, 1955), 228–29.

2. Like every part of his life, Lewis's atheism and subsequent experience of conversion have been discussed and dissected by numerous authors. Here, I am using George Sayer, *Jack: A Life of C. S. Lewis* (Wheaton, IL: Crossway Books, 1984), 113. For Lewis's own description of his feelings about religion at this point in his life, see Walter Hooper, ed., *They Stand Together: The Letters of C. S. Lewis to Arthur Greeves (1914–1963)* (New York: Macmillan, 1979), particularly 135–37.

3. Sayer, 217.

4. Sayer, 222–23.

5. Coghill was, like Lewis, Irish and an Oxford don. He worked most of his life to get a theatre at Oxford, and is credited with giving Richard Burton his first role. See Walter Hooper, ed., *All My Road Before Me: The Diary of C. S. Lewis 1922–1927* (New York: Harcourt Brace Jovanovich Publishers, 1991), 462.

6. Lewis, *Joy,* 212–15.

7. Ibid., 191.

8. Ibid., 204–05.

9. Ibid., 208–11.

10. David C. Downing, *The Most Reluctant Convert: C. S. Lewis's Journey to Faith* (Downers Grove, IL: InterVarsity Press, 2002), 132–33.

11. William Griffin, *Clive Staples Lewis: A Dramatic Life* (San Francisco: Harper & Row, Publishers, 1986), 52–53.

12. Downing, 135.

13. Lewis, *Joy,* 215–28.

14. Ibid., 230–31.

15. C. S. Lewis, *The Weight of Glory* (New York: Harper Collins Publishers, Inc., 1980), 28.

16. Ibid., 34.

17. Sayer, 225.

18. Lewis, *Joy,* 233–36.

19. Sayer, 225–26. Downing remarks that this date marks the midpoint of Jack's life, since he died on November 22, 1963. But, Downing says, "If it took him longer than most people to hammer out his worldview, the one he forged was one of matchless intellectual vitality and imaginative beauty." Downing, 155.

20. Sayer, pp. 225–26; Lewis, *Joy,* 237.

21. Hooper, *They Stand,* 426–27.

22. Ibid., 427. Hooper points out in a footnote that Tolkien's long poem *Mythopoena* is his own account of this interesting conversation.

23. Downing, 18, 159. Downing also remarks that Lewis's years as an unbeliever made him particularly effective as a Christian apologist: He understood atheism. Downing, 15.

24. Donald E. Glover, *C. S. Lewis: The Art of Enchantment* (Athens, OH: Ohio University Press, 1981), 10.

25. Lewis, *Joy,* 238.

26. Hooper, *They Stand,* 430.

27. Erik Routley, "A Prophet," in James T. Coco, ed., *C. S. Lewis at the Breakfast Table and Other Reminiscences,* rev. ed.

C. S. Lewis and Human Suffering

(Orlando, FL: Harcourt Brace Jovanovich, Publishers, 1992), 26. Routley was reacting to Lewis's sermon "The Weight of Glory," which he delivered on June 8, 1941, at the Church of St. Mary the Virgin at Oxford University. See also C. S. Lewis, *"The Weight of Glory" and Other Addresses,* rev. ed. (New York: Harper Collins Publishers, Inc., 2001), 25–46.

    28. Alan Bede Griffiths, "The Adventures of Faith," in James T. Coco, ed., *C. S. Lewis at the Breakfast Table and Other Reminiscences,* rev. ed. (Orlando, FL: Harcourt Brace Jovanovich, Publishers, 1992), 17, 19, 24; quotation on p. 17. Griffiths had Lewis as a tutor at Oxford. When they first met, neither was Christian. Griffiths later became a Catholic and their relationship cooled.

    29. Griffin, *Clive Staples Lewis,* 53.

    30. From a letter Lewis wrote to Arthur Greeves, February 1932. See Hooper, *They Stand,* 438–39. Cited in Griffin, 84.

    31. Armand M. Nicholi, *The Question of God: C. S. Lewis and Sigmund Freud Debate God, Love, Sex, and The Meaning of Life* (New York: The Free Press, 2002), 77.

    32. Glover, 18, 24, 25.

    33. Austin Farrer, "The Christian Apologist," in Jocelyn Gibb, ed., *Light on C. S. Lewis* (New York: Harcourt Brace Jovanovich, 1965), 23–24.

    34. Ibid., 25, 26.

    35. Ibid., 28, 31. Publishing information about these Lewis books can be found in the Bibliography.

    36. C. S. Lewis, *Letters to Malcolm: Chiefly on Prayer* (New York: Harcourt Brace Jovanovich Paperback, 1973), 140.

    37. Chad Lewis, "The Impact on America," in Gibb, 110–11.

    38. Sayer, 291. Sayer goes on to recount Jack's tremendous sadness at Williams' death in 1945, but, at the same time, his strong sense of Williams' continued presence. This deepened Jack's faith and moved him to believe in life after death. It was also Williams who introduced Lewis to the theory of substitution, which later

moved Jack to offer himself as a substitute in Joy's place when she was suffering the pain of her cancer. Sayer, 295.

39. Coghill, in Gibb, 63.

40. Michael White, *C. S. Lewis: Creator of Narnia* (New York: Carroll & Graf Publishers, 2005), 167.

41. Sayer, 205. See C. S. Lewis, *The Great Divorce* (New York: Macmillan Publishing Company, 1946).

42. Downing, 120.

43. Downing, 123, 130. Downing is relying here on C. S. Lewis, *Pilgrim's Regress* Reprint (New York: Harcourt Brace Jovanovich, 1966).

44. C. S. Lewis, *The Case for Christianity* (New York: Collier Books, 1989), 25.

45. Ibid., 27.

46. C. S. Lewis, *God in the Dock: Essays on Theology and Ethics,* Walter Hooper, ed. (Grand Rapids, MI: William B. Eerdmans Publishing Company, 1970), 12.

4. The Problem of Pain

1. C. S. Lewis, *Letters to Malcolm: Chiefly on Prayer* (New York: Harcourt, Inc., 1992), 41–43.

2. C. S. Lewis, *A Grief Observed* (New York: HarperCollins Publishers, 1994), 87.

3. C. S. Lewis, *The Problem of Pain* (New York: Touchstone, 1996), 10.

4. Lewis, *Problem,* p. viii. Cited in George Sayer, *Jack: A Life of C. S. Lewis* (Wheaton, IL: Crossway Books, 1988), 270.

5. Walter Hooper, ed., *Letters of C. S. Lewis,* rev. ed. (Fount Paperbacks, 1998). Cited in Walter Hooper, *C. S. Lewis: Companion & Guide* (San Francisco: Harper San Francisco, 1996), 295.

6. Lewis, *Problem,* 28–29.

7. Ibid., 12, 14, 21; quotation on p. 14.

8. C. S. Lewis, *God in the Dock: Essays on Theology and Ethics,* Walter Hooper, ed. (Grand Rapids, MI: William B. Eerdmans Publishing Company, 1970), 224–25.

9. Lewis, *Problem,* 32.

10. Sayer, 321.

11. Armand M. Nicholi, *The Question of God: C. S. Lewis and Sigmund Freud Debate God, Love, Sex, and The Meaning of Life* (New York: The Free Press, 2002), 103–4. Nicholi contrasts Lewis's approach to pain with that of Freud's, whose nonspiritual world-view could give no comfort, only resignation. Freud, then, is like the "pre-*joy*" Lewis. Nicholi, 213–14.

12. Lewis, *Problem,* 33, 35–36, 43; quotation on p. 33.

13. Austin Farrer, "The Christian Apologist," in Jocelyn Gibb, *Light on C. S. Lewis* (New York: Harcourt Brace Jovanovich, 1965), 36.

14. Thanks are due to Addison Wright, SS, for his courses in scripture over several summers. See also Bernhard W. Anderson, *Understanding the Old Testament,* 5th ed. (Upper Saddle River, NJ: Pearson/Prentice Hall, 2007), 539–51.

15. C. S. Lewis, ed., *Essays Presented to Charles Williams* (London: Oxford University Press, 1947). Cited in Hooper, *Companion,* 295.

16. Harold S. Kushner, *When Bad Things Happen to Good People* (New York: Avon Books, 1981).

17. Ibid. This comes from chapter 2, "The Story of a Man Named Job," 31–45.

18. Ibid., 38.

19. Ibid., 38–43, quotation on p. 43. As my students have on occasion pointed out, the readers of Job, who know why he suffers, are in the position to do this sort of reasoning. His wife and friends doubted the truth of Statement C.

20. Ibid., 60.

21. Ibid., 102–3.

22. Lewis, *Problem,* 83–85.

23. Ibid., 85–86.

24. Ibid., 91, 93–95.

25. C. S. Lewis, *Surprised by Joy: The Shape of My Early Life* (New York, Harcourt, Brace & Company, 1955), 170–71.

26. C. S. Lewis, *Reflections on the Psalms* (New York: Harvest Books, 1986), 12, 39–43.

5. I Shall Never Be a Biped Again

1. Copied personally by the author at Joy's burial place in the Oxford Crematorium, in Spring 2002. The often-cited inscription is actually a reworking of Lewis's early poem "Epitaph," which Joy liked so much that she requested he write a new version to be used for her memorial.

2. C. S. Lewis, *A Grief Observed* (San Francisco: Harper San Francisco, 1994), 19. Further references to the book in this chapter are cited in parentheses in the text itself.

3. Douglas H. Gresham, *Lenten Lands: My Childhood with Joy Davidman and C. S. Lewis* (San Francisco: Harper San Francisco, 1988), 130–31. Gresham adds that the book "cost Jack great pain and yet rewarded him with deeper understanding."

4. Armand M. Nicholi, *The Question of God: C. S. Lewis and Sigmund Freud Debate God, Love, Sex, and the Meaning of Life* (New York: The Free Press, 2002), 210. Nicholi also sees Joy's death as bringing back for Lewis everything he felt at the loss of his mother. Austin Ferrar goes so far as to question how we can "take [the book] *The Problem of Pain* seriously," in light of *A Grief Observed.* Once Lewis lost Joy, he realized that his intellectual theories were no help at all. See Austin Ferrar, "The Christian Apologist," in Jocelyn Gibb, ed., *Light on C. S. Lewis* (New York: Harcourt Brace Jovanovich, 1965), 31.

5. Lewis, *Surprised by Joy,* 212.

6. Cited in John Ryan Duncan, *The Magic Never Ends: The Life and Works of C. S. Lewis* (Nashville, TN: W Publishing Group, 2001), 157. Christopher Mitchell is assistant professor of theology and director of the Marion Wade Center at Wheaton College in Illinois, which holds a major collection of Lewis papers.

7. Sources about C. S. Lewis are abundant, and there are sources, too, about Joy Davidman.

8. Walter Hooper, *C. S. Lewis: Companion & Guide* (San Francisco: Harper San Francisco, 1996), 197.

9. Hooper, 194.

10. Ibid., 194–95. Hooper notes that some readers, who did not guess the real author, actually sent copies to Lewis, thinking it would help him as it had helped them. After Lewis's own death, *A Grief Observed* was finally published under his own name.

11. C. S. Lewis, *Mere Christianity* [American Edition] (New York: The Macmillan Company, 1960). In the 1993 movie *Shadowlands,* this is emphasized by the "canned" speech Lewis gives to any number of diverse groups who seek him out as a guest lecturer. The words later come back to haunt him as friends tried to comfort him with the same assurances.

12. Some authors seem to feel the need to "defend" Lewis against claims that *A Grief Observed* shows a man losing his faith. Michael White, however, observes that it was never Lewis's faith that was threatened, but his view of God: God existed but was not good; rather God was a cruel deity who enjoyed playing with humans. See Michael White, *C. S. Lewis: Creator of Narnia* (New York: Carroll & Graf Publishers, 2005), 201.

6. An Approach to Mourning

1. W. H. Lewis, ed., *Letters of C. S. Lewis* (New York: Harcourt Brace Jovanovich, 1966), 206. Cited in Robert F. Morneau,

A Retreat with C. S. Lewis: Yielding to a Pursuing God (Cincinnati: St. Anthony Messenger Press, 1999), 91–92.

2. The ritual would, of course, have to be modified for those Christians whose denomination does not incorporate communion as part of the final ministry to the dying.

3. Jane Marks, "Comforting the Grieving," *Good Housekeeping* (January 1998), 68.

4. I am grateful to Alan Wolfelt, founder of the Center for Loss & Life Transition in Fort Collins, Colorado, for his extended workshop—Comprehensive Bereavement Skills Training, June 2002.

5. Quoted in Sheldon Vanauken, *A Severe Mercy* (New York: Bantam Books, 1979), 184. The letter is dated February 10, 1955.

6. This is what Wolfelt calls "grief bursts."

7. Only the Life I've Led

1. William Griffin, *Clive Staples Lewis: A Dramatic Life* (San Francisco: Harper & Row, Publishers, 1986), xxi–xxiii.

2. Owen Barfield, "Introduction," in Jocelyn Gibb, ed., *Light on C. S. Lewis* (New York: Harcourt Brace Jovanovich, 1965), xiii. Owen Barfield was a London solicitor and a member of the Inklings. Although they held differing opinions on many topics, Lewis and Barfield were great friends and truly respected each other. See Colin Duriez and David Porter, *The Inklings Handbook: The lives, thought and writings of C. S. Lewis, J. R. R. Tolkien, Charles Williams, Owen Barfield and their friends* (St. Louis, MO: Chalice Press, 2001).

3. C. S. Lewis, *Letters to an American Lady,* Clyde S. Kilby, ed. (Grand Rapids, MI: William B. Eerdmans Publishing Company, 1967), 111.

4. George Sayer, *Jack: A Life of C. S. Lewis* (Wheaton, IL: Crossway Books, 1988), 205.

5. John Constable, aware of the negative attitude of many at Oxford toward Lewis's "popular" works, remarks that the years at Cambridge later in Lewis's career may have been his happiest, since at that time Cambridge was "far less skeptical about Lewis's brand of religious popularization than Oxford." John Constable, "C. S. Lewis: from Magdalen to Magdalene," *Magdalene College Magazine and Record* 32 (1988), 42–46.

6. Michael White, *C. S. Lewis: Creator of Narnia* (New York: Carroll & Graf Publishers, 2005), 225.

7. This is taken from a eulogy Farrer delivered at a memorial service for Lewis in Magdalen College on December 7, 1963. Later, Farrer included the eulogy, under the title "In His Image: In Commemoration of C. S. Lewis," in his book *The Brink of Mystery* (London: SPCK, 1976). Cited in Walter Hooper, *C. S. Lewis: Companion & Guide* (San Francisco: Harper San Francisco, 1996), 120.

Bibliography

Abrams, M. H., gen. ed. *William Wordsworth: The Complete Poetical Works*. London: Macmillan and Co., 1888.

Anderson, Bernhard W. *Understanding the Old Testament,* 5th ed. Upper Saddle River, NJ: Pearson/Prentice Hall, 2007.

Chisham, Catherine Lynskey. "The Adventures of Aslan." *Notre Dame Magazine*. Winter 1996–1997.

Coghill, Nevill. "The Approach to English." In *Light on C. S. Lewis,* edited by Jocelyn Gibb. New York: Harcourt Brace Jovanovich, 1965.

Constable, John. "C. S. Lewis: From Magdalen to Magdalene." *Magdalene College Magazine and Record* 32 (1988): 42–46.

Davidman, Joy. "The Longest Way Round." In *These Found the Way: Thirteen Converts to Protestantism,* edited by David Wesley Soper. Philadelphia: Westminster Press, 1951.

Dorsett, Lyle W. *A Love Observed: Joy Davidman's Life & Marriage to C. S. Lewis.* Wheaton, IL: Harold Shaw Publishers, 1998.

Downing, David C. *The Most Reluctant Convert: C. S. Lewis's Journey to Faith.* Downers Grove, IL: InterVarsity Press, 2002.

Duncan, John Ryan. *The Magic Never Ends: The Life and Works of C. S. Lewis.* Nashville, TN: W Publishing Group, 2001.

Duriez, Colin, and David Porter. *The Inklings Handbook: The lives, thought and writings of C. S. Lewis, J. R. R. Tolkien, Charles Williams, Owen Barfield and their friends.* St. Louis, MO: Chalice Press, 2001.

Farrer, Austin. "The Christian Apologist." In *Light on C. S. Lewis,* edited by Jocelyn Gibb. New York: Harcourt Brace Jovanovich, 1965.

Fussell, Paul. *The Great War and Modern Memory.* Oxford, NY: Oxford University Press, 1975.

Gibb, Jocelyn, ed. *Light on C. S. Lewis.* New York: Harcourt Brace Jovanovich, 1965.

Gilchrist, K. J. *A Morning after War: C. S. Lewis and WWI.* New York: Peter Lang, 2005.

Glover, Donald E. *C. S. Lewis: The Art of Enchantment.* Athens, OH: Ohio University Press, 1981.

Gresham, Douglas. *Jack's Life: The Life Story of C. S. Lewis.* Nashville, TN: Broadman & Holman Publishers, 2005.

―――――. *Lenten Lands: My Childhood with Joy Davidman and C. S. Lewis.* San Francisco: Harper San Francisco, 1988.

Griffin, William. *Clive Staples Lewis: A Dramatic Life.* San Francisco: Harper & Row, Publishers, 1986.

Hooper, Walter, ed. *All My Road Before Me: The Diary of C. S. Lewis 1922–1927.* New York: Harcourt Brace Jovanovich, Publishers, 1991.

―――――. *C. S. Lewis: Companion and Guide.* San Francisco: Harper San Francisco, 1996.

―――――, ed. *Letters of C. S. Lewis.* Rev. Ed. Fount Paperbacks, 1998.

―――――. *They Stand Together: The Letters of C. S. Lewis to Arthur Greeves (1914–1963).* New York: Macmillan Publishing Co., Inc., 1979.

Kushner, Harold S. *When Bad Things Happen to Good People.* New York: Avon Books, 1981.

Lawlor, John. *C. S. Lewis: Memories and Reflections.* Dallas, TX: Spence, 1999.

Lewis, C. S. *The Case for Christianity.* New York: Collier Books, 1989.

Bibliography

_____. *The Collected Letters of C. S. Lewis, Vol. 1: Family Letters 1905–1931*. London: HarperCollins, 2000.

_____, ed. *Essays Presented to Charles Williams*. London: Oxford University Press, 1947.

_____. *God in the Dock: Essays on Theology and Ethics*. Walter Hooper, ed. Grand Rapids, MI: William B. Eerdmans Publishing Company, 1970.

_____. *The Great Divorce*. New York: MacMillan Publishing Company, 1946.

_____. *A Grief Observed*. San Francisco: Harper San Francisco, 1994.

_____. *Letters to an American Lady*. Clyde S. Kilby, ed. Grand Rapids, MI: William B. Eerdmans Publishing Company, 1967.

_____. *Letters to Dom Bede Griffiths, Vol. 1 (1931–1948)*. Marion Wade Center. Wheaton College. Wheaton, IL.

_____. *Letters to Malcolm: Chiefly on Prayer*. Orlando, FL: Harcourt, Inc., 1992.

_____. *Pilgrim's Regress*. Reprint. New York: Harcourt Brace Jovanovich, 1966.

_____. *The Problem of Pain*. New York: Touchstone, 1996.

_____. *Reflection on the Psalms*. New York: Harvest Books, 1986.

_____. *Spirits in Bondage: A Cycle of Lyrics*. Walter Hooper, ed. San Diego: Harcourt Brace & Company, 1984.

_____. *Surprised by Joy: The Shape of My Early Life*. San Diego: Harcourt Brace & Company, 1955.

_____. *The Weight of Glory*. New York: Harper Collins Publishers, Inc., 1980.

_____. *The Weight of Glory and Other Addresses*. Rev. Ed. New York: Harper Collins Publishers, Inc., 2001.

Lewis, W. H., ed. *Letters of C. S. Lewis*. New York: Harcourt Brace Jovanovich, 1966.

Marks, Jan. "Comforting the Grieving." *Good Housekeeping*. January 1988.

Morneau, Robert F. *A Retreat with C. S. Lewis: Yielding to a Pursuing God*. Cincinnati: St. Anthony Messenger Press, 1999.

Morris, A. Clifford. *Miles and Miles: Some Reminiscences of an Oxford Taxi Driver and Private Car Hire Service Chauffeur*. Berkshire, Abingdon, UK: The Abbey Press, 1964.

Nicholi, Armand M. *The Question of God: C. S. Lewis and Sigmund Freud Debate God, Love, Sex, and the Meaning of Life*. New York: The Free Press, 2002.

Quiller-Couch, Arthur Thomas, ed. *The Oxford Book of English Verse 1250–1900*. Oxford: Clarendon, 1919.

Raine, Kathleen. "From a Poet." In *Light on C. S. Lewis,* edited by Jocelyn Gibb. New York: Harcourt Brace Jovanovich, 1965.

Routley, Erik. "A Prophet," In *C. S. Lewis at the Breakfast Table and Other Reminiscences,* edited by James T. Coco. Rev. Ed. Orlando, FL: Harcourt Brace Jovanovich, Publishers, 1992.

Sayer, George. *Jack: A Life of C. S. Lewis*. Wheaton, IL: Crossway Books, 1988.

Sibley, Brian. *C. S. Lewis Through the Shadowlands: The Story of His Life with Joy Davidman*. Grand Rapids, MI: Fleming H. Revell, 1994.

Vanauken, Sheldon. *A Severe Mercy*. New York: Bantam Books, 1979.

Watson, George, ed. *Critical Essays on C. S. Lewis*. Aldershot, UK: Scolar Press, 1992.

White, Michael. *C. S. Lewis: Creator of Narnia*. New York: Carroll & Graf Publishers, 2005.